MW00634880

A HANDBOOK FOR LOVE

Alexandra Mason, Ph.D.

Photo credits:

Cloud heart: 5536649©Yoyo1972/Dreamstime.com

Heart stones: 1803212©SergetGalushko/Dreamstime.com

Red heart tree: 87962375©creativecommonstockphoto/Dreamstime.com

Bleeding heart: 95476935©creativecommonstockphoto/Dreamstime.com

Tiny objects: 82988578©creativecommonstockphoto/Dreamstime.com

Heart leaf: 750470©MaryKatherineWynn/Dreamstime.com

Smoke as heart: 169963©JamesKnopf/Dreamstime.com

Apple as heart: 17273302©MorganOliver/Dreamstime.com

Tulips as heart: 4621254©creativecommonphotos/Dreamstime.com

Rope knot as heart: 10701145©creativecommonphotos/Dreamstime.com

Heart around globe: 6075959©Rudat/Dreamstime.com

Birds make heart: 5673595©AnatolySamara/Dreamstime.com

Shell heart: 2159934©PetraWanski/Dreamstime.com

Other photos in public domain.

Dedicated to my sister, Karen

©by Alexandra Mason, 2022
Turnstone Books of Oregon, LLC
ISBN 978-1-7373958-2-9
Turnstone logo courtesy of Pepper Trail

"Love is the only sane and satisfactory answer to the problem of human existence."

—Erich Fromm

CONTENTS

The subject tonight is Love
And for tomorrow night as well,
As a matter of fact
I know of no better topic
For us to discuss
Until we all
Die!
—Hafiz

"Where there is no love, pour love in, and you will draw love out."

"In the twilight of life, God will not judge us on our earthly possessions and human success, but rather on how much we have loved."
—San Juan de la Cruz

THE UNIVERSALITY OF LOVE, OR A LETTER TO EVERYONE BEFORE IT'S TOO LATE

"Love one another and you will be happy. It's as simple and as difficult as that."—Michael Leunig

If you are reading this now, you must know that I have always loved you.

Perhaps our paths have crossed. If I saw you when you were a child, I instantly, instinctively, prayed for all good circumstances in your upbringing. I wished you wonder at learning about our human basics—about the warmth of a parental hug, about letters that squiggle across a page, about what makes each of us giggle with delight. I wished you mostly good health, with just enough of small maladies to make you appreciate being well.

I wished you safety and safety nets—good intuition in handling the cowardly bully, care crossing streets, a fostering neighborhood and loving aunts, uncles, cousins. I wished you joy in your schooling and success in at least one thing—solving tough puzzles, telling a good joke, hitting a strong line drive. I wished you acceptance of your body however it may be and of your irascible hair that refuses to stay in your cap. I wished you trustworthy friends and good friendships. I wished you the opportunity to speak candidly and be yourself.

If you lived in a struggling country, I wished you nourishment and freedom from strife. I hoped harm would let you be a child without the worries of adulthood before their time.

If I passed you on a city street, I wondered what was on your mind. My heart leapt into yours. Maybe you sensed this, and our eyes met. Perhaps a fleeting small smile passed between us. Were you worried about your mother's failing health, the slow creep of a genetic dementia? Did you wonder how you would survive a workplace vexed with power plays and make it home late with groceries for the family supper? You felt trapped by limited opportunities, nothing but the same streets leading to dead ends. Yet you brushed off your jacket and clip-clopped with deliberate dignity to the bus stop. I was rooting for you. I wished you a calm serenity and the strength to persevere.

If you were my student, I placed you above everything. I took you seriously. I wanted to tell you things we hold dear from the past, and I wanted to show you beauty. I wanted to provoke you into right choices for a satisfying life. I wanted to lead you to a precipice, and I wanted you to soar beyond where my own wings might take me. I wanted you to try, and work, and question. I hoped you would find provisional answers to all of life's dilemmas and the knowledge and reasoning to challenge your own answers and grow beyond them. I wanted you to read with empathy and thus to love the human creature. And I wanted you to create your own beautiful meanings through art.

If you were ever part of my family, words cannot describe my loyal bond to you. If you are my kin, I have always known we are kindred, tied by invisible elements of blood, matter, ancestry. As children we played at everything together. We schooled, we doctored, we kept house, we staged gunfights, we conquered the mountain-hillock, we chased each other and kissed, we danced, we dropped pennies down the well and watched the ripples spread. We tried to smoke cigarettes. We argued—Is not! Is too! We stuffed our cheeks with ripe raspberries from prodigious vines. We gave each other driving lessons.

And then we went our separate ways—yet as news of family illness, divorce, death reached us, my love for you was always reaffirmed. Maybe we inhabit markedly different realms now. Some of us studied, some served, some became worshippers or outcasts. Maybe we speak different idioms now. Some of us were parents; some of us loved animals or cultured plant life. Some of us drank ourselves into a tolerable oblivion. Some of us found one love—some of us many loves. Our tree has developed myriad shoots and seen vital roots die with our elders. Our tree is nourished by love. We will never be separated.

If you and I loved romantically, I love you now, still and to this day. Our commitment holds strong for me now as before, even if we have parted in life or through death. Maybe we seem drastically different people today with little in common, few words to share. Yet we knew one another's hearts and we threw our lots together. We cleaved unto each other—and that is always "for better." We are better for our love, and once called into being it cannot really die. When you need me, I will tend to you. My heart carries your imprint, and my life has been altered by our love.

If I met you at work or at a conference or meeting, I loved you without saying. I loved your spirit of simply being there and trying. I loved your willingness to be part of a team. When you spoke your opinion, I loved you. When you valued the creative process, I valued you. When we disagreed and worked on compromise, you were loved. When you stood up for the underdog, I admired your courage. When you lived by your convictions, my heart was moved.

Together, we live and love on this our globe, the earth.

Let us allow this love to bind us together.

LOVING EXERCISES

1. Go to a public area like a park or outdoor café or train station and take a seat. Bring along an old-fashioned or digital tablet. Settle in and use all your senses to become comfortable in the atmosphere. Then open your eyes and observe. Choose one person you can see who interests you in some way. In writing, describe that person's lovable qualities with as much imagination as needed. How and why can you love this individual?

2. Write a letter as freely as your mind will wander describing to someone moments when love for them overcame you. What were some aspects of that loving feeling? Give that person your letter or read it aloud to them.

3. Make two columns. In the first try to enumerate elements of particular instances of love you feel, as romantic love or familial love. In the second column, describe aspects of general love for humanity. Do they overlap?

LOVE IN DIFFICULT CIRCUMSTANCES

"There is no surprise more magical than the surprise of being loved." —Charles Morgan

"I have decided to stick with love. Hate is too great a burden to bear."—Martin Luther King, Jr.

"Have a great love for those who contradict and fail to love you, for in this way love is begotten in a heart that has no love." —San Juan de la Cruz

If you and I do not see eye to eye or if we've done each other wrong, I love you in spite of our differences. I had a neighbor who always seemed to be meddling. Whatever I did around the house or in the yard, he had a better idea and was sure to tell me what to do. He would offer advice on drainage and gardening and weed control. Once he told me I had a thistle in my back yard, which was fenced and not visible to him, and I should kill it now, as it was an invasive species. How he spotted this thistle remains a mystery.

But one day I had a small forsythia in a pot, and he insisted on helping me plant it. I wanted to say, "Please go away and let me work my own garden," but we dug a hole together, co-operatively, and placed the bush in the hole. Thereafter his meddling turned to more loving action. He would bring me the newspaper daily, and fetch the mail for me when it rained. Now that he has died, I'm glad I have the bright yellow flowers each spring as a reminder of him and his help—really his loving attention.

If you and I have built a wall of harsh words or ill will, or if we are separated but have never spoken, I love you through those boundaries. My sister tells of a young Chinese girl who saw her, an American traveler, an exotic stranger, near the Great Wall. The girl approached her, eyes wide, and took my sister's hand. They walked together in silence, separated by culture, experience, religion, language. The girl may have been motherless, viewing my sister, with her kindly demeanor, as a possibility. When the girl's teacher beckoned her, the girl left a coin in my sister's hand, and they have never met again. She left a token and moved a heart. Each of us finds a way, determined by spirit and circumstances. Every act is a choice. If our choices diverge or clash, it does not destroy love.

Love acknowledges disagreement and can transcend its occasional need for boundaries. To those who suffer so intensely that they desire to hurt others—to you I extend my love. Every school seems to have a bully who takes delight in taunting and even harming classmates. The will to injure—this is a shock to love. No one loves a bully, but what if someone would? The bully takes a fall from the monkey bars on the playground, and a smaller child comes over and helps him up. The child supports the bully as they make their way to the infirmary. Later, the child takes the bully's hand in hers, and the bully smiles, a bully no more.

A spark of love settling in your heart from afar has the potential to ignite love in you, if you will kindle it. But this fire is not destructive. It is the very flame of being. To burn brightly is to grow into our full potential. Love sent out returns augmented. Love always enhances the one who loves.

The power of such love is transformative. We see it in mottos, we read it in poems, we hear it in songs. All you need is love, love is the answer, love will find a way, love will keep us together, love endures all things, you'll never know how much I love you, love makes the world go 'round, how do I love thee? Let me count the ways. We seldom pause to wonder why love looms so large for all peoples, all cultures. Love we take for granted. Everyone seeks love; we all want to be loved. We sometimes throw out the phrase lightly, "Ah, I just love you for that," as if love were a rewardable action. "Love you," "Love you *more*," some say in parting, as if love is a measurable commodity.

But love cannot be a contest. It passes freely and spontaneously from one heart to another, liberating as it goes. It sees with eyes of kindness and compassion, and it bestows serenity on both the lover and the beloved.

Consider how the awareness of love can change our perspective. Each of us is the product of desire pursued and fulfilled. With hindsight we become aware of the anticipation for us as individuals from the prior generations. They planned for us; they awaited us; they welcomed us; they reared us. They prayed that our lives would be even better than theirs. We see this in their documentation of our being: our birth announcements, photographic treasures, lines on the door jamb indicating our height at various ages. It was love that animated us and moves us along each day, even through those forebears who no longer walk the earth. Each of us is like a tree with many rings. Each ring is someone whose love invested in our becoming. We never lose these rings of connection, and they sustain us throughout our years. They are permanent markers of identity.

Sometimes the loving obligation of that connectedness challenges our capacity for giving our love freely to those who live—for love is always steadfast. But love can hurt as well as sustain, and this may be part of the cost of its ultimate benefit. If we consider family and other intimate circles, we always find accommodation. To love is to give and take, to accept and forgive. In love, we don't always get our own way, and occasionally loving requires that we suffer with or because of those we love.

The difficult or chronically ill child comes to mind. Some children seem willful or unruly to the extreme, trying the patience of a parent ultimately to tears and despair. Yet the parent cannot and does not trade the child in for another model. A loving embrace may be the simple solution. Yet some children cannot abide touching, and this poses a special challenge, reaching our heart across to them only through space. Kind words and gazes speak volumes to assure these children with a safety net of love, as well as consistent nurturing actions.

Some children come into the world with challenging disabilities, yet their parents find beauty in their being and tend to them lovingly, for their entire lives, loving through their own hurt and suffering. Their household and daily routines focus on the welfare of this loved one in need. And often they make these accommodations so readily and with such alacrity that they seem effortless, a simple matter of course for those who accept the responsibility of loving.

In some families a spouse becomes stricken with a debilitating illness and requires years of constant nursing. Somehow accommodations to ease life together begin to spring up. Wheelchair ramps, grab bars, special lift chairs and adjustable beds—these are seamlessly incorporated into home décor and used with loving attention. All who love steadfastly find in themselves an enormous capacity for giving, and in those acts they discover unmined joy. For love manifests and fulfills itself not solely in starry-eyed romantic bliss or the happiness of health and prosperity. Its true nature lies in a bittersweetness that emerges from crisis or from those moments our love is tried and tested, truly revealing our shared humanity.

My own husband found himself at the last restricted to bed because of an inability to breathe without an oxygen machine. One day in a February I returned home from shopping to find a vase filled with two dozen red roses. I smilingly asked him where the flowers came from, and he said, "Well, while you were gone, I got up . . . and took the car to town . . . and brought these roses home . . . just for you." Of course we both knew this was an impossible series of events. He actually had arranged with the housekeeper to do this on the sly—but the lovingness of the gesture was even more poignant through his disability. His act also gave joy to his conspirator, as she later recounted driving by several times until she was sure I was away from the house, and the fun she had in arranging the blooms to the delight of my husband.

The warmth of love that we feel through sorrowful circumstances grows our own hearts, increasing our capacity for loving in the world. We may find that families challenged by troubled times often seem the happiest, filled with great aptitude and facility for love.

LOVING EXERCISES

1. Describe a time in your life when you found it difficult to express love. Was the obstacle in you, or was there a person who made it seemingly hard to love them? What makes a person hard to love?

2. Try to remember an event in your life when you let a feeling of resentment or revenge or injustice block your feelings of love. How can we deal with carrying a grudge? How might we react differently?

3. Imagine that you are in a public place and see an elderly man being bullied. How might you approach the man and/or the bully to defuse the situation?

MANY FACETS OF LOVE

"The soul that walks in love neither tires others nor grows tired."—San Juan de la Cruz

While love is a genuine and vividly-felt human emotion, we are often awkward or uncertain about how to show our love. Self-consciousness can lead us into self-doubt. Instead of freely and genuinely sharing our joy of loving, we falter. Will the emotion overwhelm? Might we be rejected? Do others feel as we do? And can I find the person "meant" for me?

Novels, poems, songs, and movies have offered an array of conventions for romantic and familial love, especially. We do experience genuine feelings, but then how are we to move ahead? We are given others' words of love. We are shown love gifts—flowers, fine chocolates, pre-written cards. We see happy family gatherings, camping trips, smiles and smooches and hugs. Art and media have taught us ways to show love, which unfortunately have become normative. We hold false ideals of how love plays out, how it should and must be, and we are more than frequently disappointed.

Family gatherings often fall into bickering and quarrelling when a vision of harmony does not unfold as envisioned. Or take a look at the self-presentation ads on any match-maker dating site, and you will find iterations of the idyllic love-dream: holding hands, long walks on the beach, country drives, sitting by the cozy fire. All these external correlatives for a loving relationship, aside from being rare activities in actuality, are simply on the wrong path. Their focus is outward rather than inward, on receiving rather than giving, on the "forms" of love rather than the action of loving.

The formula for love emanates from within, and it begins with ourselves. Love is an action or activity in that it must become for each of us a default outlook on life. When we embody love, when we radiate love, all else follows: everything falls into place. Our dreams can come true.

It's no surprise that we are culturally conditioned into expectations for love, but these lessons often limit and stifle us, which can lead to a personal history of profound frustration. As the country song observes, we may be "looking for love in all the wrong places." The very fact that so many of us "seek" love, as something that will be attained or accomplished, pinpoints our error. Loving is a way of being, not a blue-ribbon prize, and it is a verb rather than a noun. We "find" love when we discover love within ourselves and practice it daily. Romantic partnership is an extension of this process. We open ourselves to the love that animates our very being; we know and accept and care for ourselves, body and soul; we bring a loving attitude to every human encounter; and we experience a unity of this force with certain others as our spirits bridge the gap of separate selfhood. *Namaste'*: the spirit in me recognizes the spirit in you. I love you.

I have two friends whose history for at least a decade has been a failed and frustrated search for "true love." In experiencing these frustrations and failures, both have allowed themselves to become cynical and even whiny about no one loving them— which, ironically, makes them even less lovable. My woman friend posts blogs for the world to see on the internet about her loneliness on holidays, about her jealousy of others whom she perceives as having perfect family lives or idyllic romantic love, about the tragic suffering of people in her position, alone. Implicit is a resentful sense of blame projected outwards.

One feels the call for help, certainly, but advice is met with excuses: I've already tried that, fate has dealt me a lousy hand, why me? The focus is always on lack of receiving or having, rather than opening the heart, reaching out, living in an attitude of loving self and life and thus loving others. To love might be to receive the love she longs for.

My male friend suffers from substance addiction and persists in seeking a partner who supports the idea of joy in "partying," a kind of aimless and constant inebriation. His self-chosen motto is "Good Times," and his philosophy that one should "Work to Live"—where "living" consists of a monotonous sameness of casual relationships in an idle silliness of belches and giggles and frantic smoking of cigarettes. Now, after three failed relationships built on these ideas, his health has failed too and he's decades past the carefree days of teenage. He scours the internet for partners, basing his evaluation on looks and acceptance of his philosophy. Fewer and fewer candidates respond to his offering as attractive, and he wallows deeper and deeper in his isolation.

Old friends have married and grown families and moved on from his mindset of the carefree adolescent life. He has developed no passion to sustain his own personal life, looking only for the temporary validation of camaraderie in revelry. He can practice the gestures of love he's seen in our culture, giving flowers, buying gifts, treating to dinners and drinks. Yet these remain empty rituals because they are not generated by loving, only by

18

the desire to be loved and to enact the "forms" of love for others to admire.

Like my woman friend, he is resentful of others who seem to have achieved all he lacks. So he takes pains to tear them down—rather than to build love from within himself. She didn't love me enough. What did I do wrong? He constantly wonders. Counseling has supplied frameworks for self-understanding and growth, yet he scoffs at these—and continues to avoid essential self-care, the character to reach out truly from the heart to discover love. Sadly, it seems that in all these relationships he has never truly experienced love—by loving.

Our society is filled with these tragic stories. Decades pass in a restless and resentful unhappiness for those who chase love without catching it, and then blame love itself. First we must realize that we will not channel all our love into just one person. Love by definition is characterized by largesse, by an embarrassment of riches. So particular love, an intimate relationship, must emanate from the foundational love of being, which will always overspill its boundaries—for it animates the universe, makes us human. The most validating love expression I've received was when my partner declared I was his "élan vital," the force or impulse for life. As ironic as it might seem, loving in the world must begin with a validation of this force within ourselves.

When we acknowledge and accept the love of creation within ourselves, we become enabled to spread and share that love, for it links up the very vibrancy of being across physical boundaries. And loving will enrich our lives in many guises. We will have long-time loving friendships; we will have the familial love of kin and clan, of parents and blood relatives; we will experience young love and mature love and even love from afar. What links all these is the capability of putting another person first. To love is to share responsibility for that relationship, to be accountable to ourselves and the loved one. And to commit to loving, constantly, daily.

Like essential ingredients in a scrumptious recipe, loving subdivides into those elements bell hooks emphasizes in *All About Love*: "care, affection, . . . respect, commitment, and trust." It's easy to perceive how these extend outward from the love we find first in our own being. Loving enhances ourselves, but it is not about ourselves. It is the extension of self into nurturing another. By being selfless, we become most fully ourselves.

Moreover, we must not fear first being alone in productive self-examination that centers us, situates us to be loving, by finding the universal love that gave us the spark of life. Self-knowledge and a humble acceptance of our own humanity are essential to loving. Before we can offer these to others, we must care for our personal well-being, like ourselves and laugh at ourselves, have respect for our own moral choices, and be of good character so that we are trustworthy and reliable.

Such centering makes us neither smug, cynical, arrogant, nor complacent. Rather, we discover both humility and patience in loving and accepting ourselves. To succumb to cynicism about love in our complex modern world is to negate it before even trying. Loving is always optimistic and hopeful. It trusts to time to reveal love's riches, love's largesse, yet this hopeful confidence sees beneath and beyond the often deceptive idealized formulae for LOVE. Love is never perfect, yet it is always a form of perfection—the best of being human. Loving, like patience, is its own reward. Tended to consistently, nurtured, like a garden, the result will be beautifully surprising, no doubt different from our plans, and always soul-filling, profoundly satisfying.

LOVING EXERCISES

1. Devote a month to a selfless volunteer action in the community. Write down how this service makes you feel.

2. Practice ten random acts of loving kindness and record them in your journal, along with your reaction to them.

3. Meditate for ten minutes a day on inner love. Try to feel to the core of your being the purity of your spark of life.

SELF-LOVE AS A FOUNDATION

"You yourself, as much as anybody in the entire universe, deserve your love and affection."—Buddha

"There are two basic motivating forces: fear and love. When we are afraid, we pull back from life. When we are in love, we open to all that life has to offer with passion, excitement, and acceptance. We need to learn to love ourselves first, in all our glory and our imperfections. If we cannot love ourselves, we cannot fully open to our ability to love others or our potential to create. Evolution and all hopes for a better world rest in the fearlessness and open-hearted vision of people who embrace life." —John Lennon

We carry a foundational love inside of us, and this ignites self-love. Our birth itself is a sign of value. We learn more of our personal worthiness as we experience love from others—all of our teachers, all of our nurturers. We may receive unexpected acts of pure love from strangers or sages. It is when we accept self-worth that we begin to light up our world. Self-love is recognizing the creative force of being within ourselves. *Namasté*, say the Buddhists, the spirit within me recognizes the spirit within you.

Self-love is not an aggressive projection of ego onto the world. It is a serenity of existence, full being here now, an investment in each moment of our participation in humanity. When we love ourselves despite our limitations and imperfections, we can empathize with all others in a similar condition, and we love, unconditionally.

When we feel centered, we will live mindfully, forging a consistency between our selfhood and our actions in the world. The romantic side of us may desire to live "freely," to decide everything as we go along. But too many choices can become an enormous burden—and not every little thing needs to be a daily decision. This would exhaust even the strongest among us. Mindfulness requires a kind of self-discipline that results in habits that carry us along. Mindful living understands that we must BOTH live fully in the moment AND plan for tomorrow and tomorrow and tomorrow. Our mental state is, in a way, grounded in our physicality.

Younger people are often amazed, maybe even scornful, of the habits of the elderly, who may in fact thrive because of their self-discipline. These masters of living rise about the same time each day and begin a standard routine. My mother always started her day by sitting at the table and drinking a large tumbler of water. Others immediately take a brief walk or tidy up the bedroom or write a list of tasks or a journal entry. Oregon poet William Stafford is famous for his early-morning writing regimen, day after day, whether he produced a finished poem or not. In larger cities we see groups of people who have gathered together in parks to practice yoga or t'ai chi as a self-loving habit to begin their day.

The great cellist Pablo Casals attributes his success to this sort of self-disciplined approach to time informed by habit:

> Each day I am reborn. Each day I must begin again. For the past eighty years I have started each day in the same manner. . . not a mechanical routine but something essential to my daily life. I go to the piano, and I play two preludes and fugues of Bach. I cannot think of doing otherwise. It is a sort of benediction on the house. But that is not its only meaning for me. It is a rediscovery of the world of which I have the joy of being a part. It fills me with awareness of the wonder of life, with a feeling of the incredible marvel of being a human being.

> The music is never the same for me, never. Each day is something new, fantastic, unbelievable. That is Bach, like nature, a miracle!

A daily routine does not dull the new day; on the contrary, the routine enables us to experience the joy of beginning again.

Morning also requires nourishment. Those living mindfully consider the day's meals and perhaps begin preliminary preparations for later. Planning leads to a balance and regularity of diet, with mindful and economical attention paid to shopping and storing of fresh foodstuffs. Many of us are tempted to "just pick something up," the fast-food habit that results in high intake of empty calories. And, instead of nutrition, some of us have come to see high-calorie foods as well-deserved treats, not acknowledging that we are working counter to good self-love when we indulge ourselves constantly. I have friends who must visit the refrigerator each time they return home, no matter the time of day, an action they find comforting. Much of our tendency to over-indulgence comes from doing a thing automatically, unmindfully.

If mindfulness leads to discipline, in turn these combine to help create within us a depth of inner resources. Over time our routines develop into a deep certainty and confidence in who we are, and this self-integration sustains us in times of challenge and hardship. If we hold a sense that all will be well through how we habitually live, we need not turn to alcohol or drugs or even chocolate binges in times of stress. Popular culture has misappropriated the meaning of "me time" as just that—bingeing and over-indulgence. These prove themselves as only the most temporary of "remedies," short term feel-goods. A nourishing quiet day of me-time might instead focus on careful and pampering grooming: a soak in a hot tub, exfoliating, applying lotions, trimming of nails and hair. These prepare us to go on, an improved version of ourselves, rather than leave us feeling bloated, groggy, and hung over.

Constructive daily habits also free up time for development and pursuit of a passion, an extreme extension and expression of our selfhood. Such a passion will emanate from a combination of natural talents and proclivities developed through our particular life experience. Personal passions are nearly always constructive. They may entail planting, restoring, building, creating, cooking, challenging the self or body, studying and learning, volunteering, teaching and tutoring—the possibilities are expansive.

Those who find their passion feel an exuberance and an urge, as if they are responding to an inner mandate. And they exude an aura of joy in their passion. While the mandate is entirely personal, the passion must be shared. My favorite visits are with those who quickly say, "Let me show you . . .," and they walk visitors through a garden or a shop or a studio or a building or landscape project, or they pull out quilts or artwork or books or sit at a piano to play a new piece they've studied.

This desire to share a passion differs from those who require validation to have a sense of self. Passion stems from a strong inner life, not the need for a looking-glass self. Those who say they can't bear to spend time alone should practice just that, for both centering and self-care begin with being at home with ourselves, alone. When we experience self-acceptance by a kind of quiet reflection leading to self-knowledge, we become open to both giving and receiving love. By loving ourselves, we become beloved.

Self-love leads to love of others automatically. Self-love, in recognizing value in the tenuous fragility of individual being, instinctively generalizes that knowledge into empathy. In a sense this feeling-as-another is the source of the Golden Rule, and we might say that love, in valuing others as we value ourselves, has its primal statement in the Golden Rule.

Some version of "Do unto others as you would have them do unto you" exists in all our religions, all our sound philosophies. Some seem rewordings of the well-known Christian law, even those that predate the Biblical text. The Bahai faith says "Lay not on any soul a load that you would not wish to be laid upon you, and desire not for anyone the things you would not desire for yourself." The Buddha admonished us to "Treat not others in ways that you yourself would find hurtful." Confucius advised that "One word sums up the basis of all good conduct . . . loving-kindness. Do not do to others what you do not want done to yourself." In Hinduism, "This is the sum of duty: do not do to others what would cause pain if done to you." In the faith of Islam, according to the prophet Muhammad, "Not one of you truly believes until you wish for others what you wish for yourself." The Jains hold that "One should treat all creatures in the world as one would like to be treated."

In Jewish law, "What is hateful to you, do not do to your neighbor. This is the whole Torah." Lao Tzu established as a principle of the Tao: "Regard your neighbor's gain as your own gain and your neighbor's loss as your own loss." And even in ancient Zoroastrianism, from the second millennium BCE, "Do not do unto others whatever is injurious to yourself." Whether phrased in a positive or negative manner, the directive is identical and timeless: in action, value others as you value yourself. This is the closest our human family comes to a universal mandate.

Thus, we can cultivate the capacity to love by knowing and accepting ourselves. This requires honest social interaction but also time alone for contemplation. Self-love emanates from a kind of centering process, as in preparing to make a clay pot on a rotating wheel. In centering we clarify our individuality as expressed in our thoughts, beliefs, and actions. While people today might call this "me-time," the sages call it meditation. A confident profile then extends itself into the world through love, as a pot takes its shape, without fear of loss, harm, or compromise. However, these *will* beset the lover; they come with the territory.

Yet self-love allows us to engage in loving by assuaging our fears. When we are hurt in love or lose a loved one, the loved-self has the integrity to heal and go on. Self-love dwells in psychological mindfulness, yet it is bolstered by the body's well-being. Priests, hermits, and ascetics know the value of a practiced daily routine. Hygiene, ample nourishment, quiet contemplation or meditation, and stretching and stimulating our muscles and joints are the foundation of preparing to love. Physiologists tell us that exercise—even walking—stimulates our own "feel good" chemistry. Through body movement we produce endorphins and enhance our serotonins, both of which revitalize our mood, our outlook.

Studies indicate that happy people automatically share their happiness with those they encounter—and that, like a soft breeze that flutters the leaves on a branch, personal happiness moves through the world. It affects others; it is infectious. Happiness creates interest, like money wisely invested. Self-love becomes the source of sowing a sense of well-being everywhere we go.

Taoists conceive of our breath as life, stimulating the *chi*, which is our vital energy. Even gentle, disciplined and focused exercise can strengthen our *chi*, which we can then pass on to others as a communicative healing force. Through our palms, we feel the warmth of *chi*, and we can direct this with an electric power into those we love. Through love, we share the life-force. *Namaste'*.

My t'ai chi master Jian-ye Jiang once gave a wonderful martial arts demonstration on the big stage in McKenzie Hall at Eastern Oregon University in La Grande, Oregon. He called for a skeptic, a volunteer from the audience who did not believe in the invisible *chi*. A man came forward, and my master had him extend his hand. After centering himself through deep breaths and then movement of his own *chi* through circular hand movements, Master Jiang focused his *chi* on the man's palm and there raised beads of sweat, visible evidence of the warm passing of *chi*. The man pulled back in wonder as if shocked. *Chi* does exist, and we can stimulate and focus our own through mindful movement and meditation.

When I taught t'ai chi, I was able to perform the same demonstration for every student in my class. Although I was exhausted by the focused effort, each of them acknowledged feeling the *chi* in their palms as a received heat, an energy. I consider this a form of sharing the love, passing on our life force to another.

Although we reach out to others in love, we always must begin with ourselves. And self-love will have us instinctively love again and again, until it becomes a way of being. As Mother Teresa has said, no matter the nay-sayers, no matter the fear-mongers, no matter the result, love anyway. Just love, simply love.

LOVING EXERCISES

1. Make a list outline of things you do as a routine each day to care for yourself. Then edit the list. Might you improve on your routine? Propose changes as needed. Make sure to consider personal hygiene, sleep, exercise, meal planning and diet, housework, and meditation.

2. Abandoning humility for the moment, write down what makes you worthy of love. Why should you love yourself? Why might others love you?

3. Take a single afternoon for intense self-care, body and spirit. Soak in a shower or tub. Style your hair. Pay attention to small details of grooming. Pamper yourself. Trim hairs and nails; apply soothing lotions. Take stock of your body. Breathe deeply. Calm your mind.

PUTTING YOURSELF FIRST, THEN LAST

"If you would be loved, love, and be loveable."
—Benjamin Franklin

When I experienced a divorce from a nearly twenty-year marriage, I felt set afloat alone on a shrinking ice floe. We had fallen in love in our teens and lived two decades with joint plans for a future together, always as partners in this life. We had uprooted 3000 miles from our home turf and support groups in quest of our plans. We were each other's confidants and best friends. But our aspirations began to diverge and then overshadow the mechanics of bringing two paths together or even keeping them side by side. My husband seemed to begin seeing me as a hindrance to HIMSELF.

Such is the conundrum of preparing oneself to love. The process of putting others first ironically begins with self-examination and acceptance—but not toward an assertion of ego so intense that it builds walls of exclusion. We cannot take those who love us for granted. The civilized social graces such as kindness, courtesy, and deference to another's needs often become neglected when we move toward complacency and focus on "getting our own needs met." And this shrivels rather than nourishes even the strongest of loves. To love we must be most ourselves, but this must be the best of ourselves.

What does it mean to love ourselves? This begins with another paradox, first moving our minds outside of ourselves to the entire cosmos, whose animating force is LOVE. "God so loved the world . . . Be still, and know that I AM." Each little self carries the grandeur of creation within. The glory of such a gift obliges each of us to a responsibility to let our light shine. The world we inhabit can tend to dim that light, to dull and blunt the beauty and power of our inner radiance. We live in time, in which, as physics tells us, all things tend to inertia. Without proper attention, we may squander our time, in idleness, in carping, in base and jealous emotions, in carrying grudges, in overindulgence, in pursuing illusory and transitory pleasures—in a self-centeredness that ironically avoids knowing ourselves and caring for ourselves. Without that knowledge and care, how can we love others?

Our first obligation is husbandry, an old-fashioned word that indicates sustainable care, diligent and economical tending. We must husband both the vessel and the spirit, both our body and our soul. This basic self-care is not egocentric. Rather, it is our membership fee in the human race. No longer do most of us struggle for shelter, food, or safety, but we "owe it to ourselves" to prepare for the best, our best use of our time on earth. A centering and foundational test can inform all our personal decisions: what good comes from this action?

Finding the good for ourselves not only leads to personal happiness and welfare, a certain serenity, but in itself prepares us for love. *Mens sana in corpore sano*, a sound mind inhabits a sound body, the classic Roman poet Juvenal observed, and he advised us to pray for such a condition. With good nutrition, avoidance of noxious substances, and attention to moving all parts of our bodily vessels regularly, we can prepare the ground for our spirit and character to thrive. In a way we DECIDE to love by making the choices that reveal the love we give ourselves. Love then cannot help but to radiate outward. Like a magnet, a person who has practiced self-care attracts love and opportunities for loving.

If we've been neglecting self-care, we need not try to make a drastic change overnight. Little by little we can pay attention, be mindful of our self-damaging habits. Try a healthy nutritional diet for just two weeks and see how you feel. You can change your attitude toward food, as fuel rather than fun or reward or luxurious indulgence. A Korean-American doctor told me that he purposely ate a small portion of plain steel-cut oats with nothing added, no sugar, no milk, each morning to remind himself that food is nutrition. "Even my wife thinks I'm crazy," he said, but it is a wise craziness. He also recommended having "delicious" food only on rare occasions. That may seem overly Spartan or ascetic, but it is indeed self-care both mentally and physically, a commitment to doing something good for yourself.

It also brings us into participation with the global family of humankind. In Samuel Beckett's *Waiting for Godot*, the sadistic philosopher Pozzo remarks that "'The tears of the world are a constant quantity. For each one who begins to weep somewhere else another stops. The same is true of the laugh' *(He laughs)*." And in doing so, he deprives another person of laughter. We might say the same is true of food: for each over-indulgent portion we deprive someone else of nutrition—and this may have been the sage point of our mothers reminding us of the starving children in Asia or Africa. We are all connected, and our habits matter to humanity.

Similarly, we might add in a daily walk, even for twenty minutes, at a regular time. If you are a drinker or smoker, cut back with simple replacements (sparkling water for beer, gum or a sucker for a cigarette) and disruptions of the mechanics of a drink after work or lighting up when bored. Perhaps try a new haircut that's easy to maintain. Importantly, set aside "you time" for quiet contemplation and centering. Take stock of how your self-care is improving. Small changes add up quickly, and you will notice the differences. You will simply vibrate with vitality.

These external actions will help make profound changes to our inner life, our very character. When we know ourselves and accept ourselves, we acknowledge our own humanity and life itself as a blessing and a gift. When we accept the personal responsibility for good husbandry, practicing that self-knowledge and awareness, a calm serenity will begin to permeate our being. To do so is to accept the paradox that we will control what we can yet also be ready for the unexpected beyond our control.

A steadiness and regularity of self-care habits creates a way of life with a comforting sense of predictable rhythms. When I was first divorced, I felt it as a sign of my new personal freedom that, during my summer times off from work, I would wake each morning to a free-form day and do whatever I wanted, whatever unfolded. Ironically, this "freedom" meant too many choices, an overwhelming series of even small decisions, with the result that I felt weighed down and squandered time rather than enjoying and using it. Patterns and habits actually free up greater time—taking care of daily business without fuss and ado.

The serenity that follows leads to an enhanced patience, another irony of using our time well. *Tending to today reveals a belief in tomorrow. To be here now is an investment in the future.* Patience with the unfolding of our own lives—an acceptance of our gift of life and its mortality—will grow into patience with others, a sort of empathy for our unifying humanity. And this in turn is humbling. *Namaste'*: the spirit in me recognizes the spirit in you. In many Asian cultures, a gesture of meeting consists of folded hands and bowed heads, a reverent salute to life itself. An old-fashioned salutation or farewell was "your humble servant," a metaphor that captures this awe of being. When we best serve ourselves, we become able to extend the benevolence of life to others, and thus our world opens to the power of love. When we habitually tend to ourselves, we can then put the welfare of others BEFORE us. General love and particular love can merge in a habit we develop, of leading with love for others.

And this habit will find itself founded on the Golden Rule, that universal commandment for being human: do unto others as we would have them do unto us. With the habits of patience and humility there is no room for covetousness. We interact without competitiveness, understanding and accepting difference in our sameness. We do not feel jealousy nor do we harbor motives of revenge. All those emotions that make us perpetually unhappy disappear as with a magic eraser, when we first love ourselves and then put ourselves last.

Tending to ourselves fully, body and spirit, enhances our daily mood and outlook. When we awake with humility in an awareness of the profound gift of life, gratitude washes over every atom of our being. We take joy in a new day and a thankful delight in seeing our loved ones yet again. Morning grumpiness becomes a thing of the past. We *welcome* the morning. This may explain why religious hermits rise so very early. They are happy to be alive in the world.

In a way, to think is to be. Such an outlook becomes our default mode of action with loving as natural, second nature to ourselves. It may indeed be uncovering the godliness within. Lurking in our consciousness is the awareness that existence is fragile and fleeting. To face each day with love, for ourselves and others, is to "seize the day" and celebrate it. If we can foster and nourish a kind and loving outlook through self-care, we invite love in a continuous action that indeed confirms the godliness of the cosmos.

LOVING EXERCISES

1. Make a chart called HUSBANDRY with the categories diet, exercise, hygiene, environs, and damaging habits. Note down something you might do to improve in each category. Look at this second column each night before bedtime.

2. Think of an automatic loving phrase you can use to greet your loved ones first thing in the morning, and practice using it for at least a week. How did this affect your overall mood?

3. As you lie in bed at night with eyes closed, try to visualize your inner light, your spiritual essence. Vow that you will let it shine forth.

LOVE AS THE CREATIVE FORCE

"Love must be as much a light, as it is a flame."
—Henry David Thoreau

"At the touch of love everyone becomes a poet."
—Plato

We may actually be unable not to love—some thing, in some way. The most hardened of prisoners respond protectively and with loving concern to pets placed under their care. Such love given bolsters their own sense of self-worth. And this prepares them to return to society at large ready to extend themselves to others in at least small acts of love. Even these open to our inner potential, which is actually our creative spark.

The miracle of being human is a combination of a physical, genetic individuality with the breath of life that animates us. The creative spark of being is something we have in common. We share the same force, and it unites us in spite of ourselves. *Namasté.* The spirit in me recognizes the spirit in you. We are ourselves and the same.

Thinkers through the ages have sought the secret of life, the source of creation. While often we've conceived of this as coming from outside or above, some see each of us as carrying a piece of that creative force within us. We make comparisons to try to describe it: "This little light of mine, I'm going to let it shine." Others have imagined a cache of individual souls that enter a body at birth and vacate it at death, only to return again in another body. Famous art envisions the transference of this light, this breath, this spark or fire of being as the touch of God, as in Michelangelo's famous painting in the Sistine Chapel.

However we might envision this source, we agree that somehow our body is animated by a spirit or self that constitutes who we are. We do experience the loss of that force when someone we love dies. If you are present at the moment of someone's death, you witness the transition. When my own husband died, he exhaled his last breath, and then I felt his spirit enter me, almost as if it had floated through the air between us. There was no doubt of our love, and in this transference, real or symbolic, I felt an augmentation of self through his love.

We carry a portion of the lived life of that person in our memories. Through inspiration—literally, breathing in—from their having been, we honor their lives, as we realize the enduring power of their time on earth, their interaction with the world and with others. Sparks of the essence of their selves re-ignite our own lives: their light is passed on. We find ourselves telling their stories, whether that be a favorite joke or a life event that may even begin to assume a mythical proportion.

One day when she was a young girl, in the 1920s, my mother was riding her pony across the great open plains of southern South Dakota, when her horse shied back. She quickly spotted the problem, a coiled rattlesnake, rattles aquiver. Angry at the snake for upsetting her equine friend, she dismounted, removed the rein, and thrashed that snake to death with little thought to her own danger. As I relate this story to others, I see my own heritage and much to live up to. My mother—a tough cookie, a frontier woman—decisive and capable of heroic action. Her story teaches me what I can be, as her life is rendered vividly real through the art of story.

Further, an old friend of mine has taken this episode and given it even more significance by characterizing me as someone who tackles hard

45

tasks willfully and dutifully, "as if killing snakes." So my mother's story grows into an enduring personal mythology that, through the power of its creative force, makes a new reality. Art imitates life, said Aristotle, but in turn, life can be modeled on art.

Similarly, my nuclear family when I was a child often sang a favorite song from the 1930s, called "Brighten the Corner Where You Are." Through many listenings and singing of this, we children took all the lyrics literally to heart:

> Do not wait until some deed of
>   greatness you may do,
> Do not wait to shed your light afar.
> To the many duties ever near you
>   now be true;
> Brighten the corner where you are.

This philosophy was so integral to my parents' lives that we, the children and friends and other loved ones, sang this anthem vigorously at my mother's funeral. I've taught the song to my husband, and each day it becomes a guide to our own actions, happiness, and well-being. We honor my mother through the creative re-enactment of her theme song.

Knowing what we have learned about galaxies and the cosmos in the past fifty years by dint of space probes and powerful telescopes and modeling formulae, we may have come to think of creation on a grand scale as a matter of physics, a product of scientific dimensions and precisions. Yet the ancients spoke of hearing a perfectly-tuned cosmic operation as "the music of the spheres." One scientist, Andrew Fabian of Cambridge University, has even projected through sound wave analysis the exact tone of that perfect movement: B^b (fifty-seven octaves lower than middle C).

We can recognize moments of "hearing the music of the spheres," which becomes a metaphor for what in modern parlance we might call "being tuned in." In these moments we sense the harmony beyond ourselves on a grand and epic scale. We feel calm and "attuned" or at one with the cosmos, recognizing our small but natural and perhaps essential place within it. Some might say this is THE LOVE, the primal force, that animates us all: "God so loved the world, that He" capped his creation with the gift of his son God in man. Love is truly the foundational force.

Mental health experts (as supported by a study conducted by scientists at Stanford) recommend that we find time to position ourselves so that we might gain exposure to this harmony—by getting out of the urban landscape into the natural world. A day at the beach, a hike in the woods, time spent in a garden or park—all these settle the calmness into our spirits and minds. Seldom do we see anyone in these situations in a glum or gloomy state. Rather, the serenity we find in their Cheshire-cat-like glowing smiles reflects this perceived sense of harmony. As we allow ourselves natural time, the deeper our sense of calm oneness and belonging, until we may hear the music softly most of the time, penetrating the ordinary and mundane moments of our lives.

Those who attain this awareness we often judge as saintly, and we feel less agitated in their presence, almost as if they are tuning forks vibrating with the B^b chord. A remarkable trait of my own sister Karen was that she almost continually hummed softly. It was like the soft drone of an approaching bumblebee or the gentle whirr of a flitting hummingbird's wings. At these times she had an other-worldly look about her: she was simultaneously present in our place and time yet in harmony, hearing the song, of the creative force at work in her and everywhere. Her soft hum in turn altered her immediate world, creating a magic sound-circle of serenity.

Individually nearly every one of us finds joy in some kind of creative expression, almost in spite of ourselves. Our spirit must out. We have an innate imperative to participate in the godliness that created us and which constitutes both our uniqueness and our commonness of humanity.

This force need not be expressed on an epic scale, nor need it be widely broadcast. Early humans drew with ochre deep within the caves in which they took refuge—a private and intimate impulse. Eventually art will make itself known and be noticed. For now, brighten the corner where you are. How we design and tend to a garden, the fabrics we choose to piece together a quilt in a select pattern, the nuances we add to a lovingly-prepared meal— "No one can make it the way Grandma did!"—all these are supremely creative acts of the exuberance of spirit. Each may seem common and even ordinary, but that, in part, is their glory. Each of these activities develops from an established pattern, what we know of its prior creations, yet each enactment is as individual as its creator. Like people themselves, our creations are always different and always partaking of the same.

In this aspect, each act of creation is twice-blessed. As Shakespeare's Portia describes mercy, "It blesseth him that gives and him that takes. . . ." Whenever we manifest and share our creative spirit, it is augmented, magnified though time and space, and we reap benefits in a sort of karma, spirit that returns to us in kind. We might say that creativity, like virtue, is its own reward. But we must not underestimate the power and value of that return. We can live each day with creative spirit.

My own mother modeled twice-blessed acts of creative kindness as she aged. At seventy she would drive her older friends around on their errands, and she had an entire plan of calls to people she termed shut-ins. She scheduled creative and stimulating diversions for the elderly, talks and activities about the arts and architecture and travel. When she suffered her own dementia and lived in memory care, workers sought her out in part because her spirit so shone forth. One day I walked into her studio to find a young woman, a stranger to me, sitting on the floor with her head in my mother's lap. The young woman had responded intuitively to my mother's creative loving spirit, and she was returning the gift, twice-blessed.

We need not wonder why so many retirees turn to creative arts as they age. They carry a plenitude of spirit within for which they seek an outlet in the world. The creative spirit urges them on to write novels, poems, and memoirs; it focuses their perception of light and pattern through the lenses of their cameras; it guides their hands to dye fabrics and sketch images and melt wax into evocative swirled designs. Whether through their voices or their treasured instruments, they create joyful music. They scour the beach for nature's bounty and polish rocks into gems or turn fragments of driftwood into whimsical birdhouses.

Regardless of publicity, sales, or fame, we must see that each of these is an act of creative spirit, to share one's light with others. Everyday living is a chance to choose to be a loving force in the world. We can choose to live creatively—and be twice-blessed, no matter how small or how grand the activity.

LOVING EXERCISES

1. Describe ways in which you honor someone who has died by your own behavior and activities. What about them—character or habits—have you incorporated into your own life?

2. Seek out a place of natural beauty: the seashore, deep woods, a mountain vista. Or gaze at the sky on a starry night. Describe any feelings that pass through your body during this experience.

3. Think of how you exhibit creative actions in your own life. How do you share these acts of loving creativity with others?

SELFLESS LOVE

"One word frees us of all the weight and pain of life:
That word is love."—Sophocles

"When you plant a seed of love, it is you that
blossoms."—Ma Jaya Sati Bhagavati

Although they reap the twice-blessed benefits of their devotion, care-givers seem often to share a selfless kind of love, not seeking a return. Romantic love almost by definition wants to be requited in equal measure. Yet society thrives on the efforts of those who simply give of themselves, whose humanity prompts them to loving concern for the general welfare of others.

Hospice volunteers, for example, give their time to sit quietly and attentively with those nearing death. Their simple presence as loving, caring humans lends comfort to both the afflicted and their families. A friend of mine felt such an urgency for those approaching the end of their time on earth that she would spend hours listening to and recording stories from their lives, which she would then laboriously render into books for them and their families, permanent records of a human life lived, traces of having been.

All of us have met people who, their entire lives, have been avid volunteers. These individuals regularly give time during the week to deliver or serve up meals, to offer rides to the elderly and infirm, to read to the blind, to sing or supply live instrumental music to those in co-operative living, and so on. Some volunteer to clean up roadsides and beaches for the benefit of us all. Famously, "church women" chip in to cater and clean up for funerals—often in support of families they may not know personally.

Some choose to organize and administer non-profit gatherings to support and enhance others' quality of life in arts and educational endeavors. One may run a stable of horses offered to the severely disabled in riding therapy. Another may stage an outdoor school for youngsters, to learn to feel at home in a natural environment. Yet another helps people fill out tax forms or select insurance plans. All of these volunteers are driven, without monetary remuneration, by the highest love of all, *caritas*, a concerned sense of generous affection for and responsibility to all human beings.

What return do these who love selflessly expect? The loving—and its required investment of time—is itself the reward. Sometimes we see these activities publicly acknowledged and celebrated. A person who, with no braggadocio or fanfare, has quietly gone about loving and helping will be singled out for notice and thanks. Often we are surprised when we learn of a long history of selfless acts, for these individuals have drawn little attention to themselves. They have acted with an instinctive, and modest, sense of love.

Certain professions draw practitioners with an inner sense of *caritas*. We all know teachers who, year after year, foster students as if they were family members. We meet with and trust clergy, who, like teachers, make a small living through their selfless love. We find medical professionals who go beyond their learning and offer the healing touch of selfless love to humanity at large. I had a doctor who was originally from India. Whenever she entered the room she would gently touch my arm, and I felt as if I'd received the healing touch from Mother Teresa, as she seemed so concerned and caring, even saintly.

As President George H. W. Bush knew well, these citizens and their acts illuminate the grandeur of our culture and social well-being as "a thousand points of light." Yet the metaphor underestimates the number and power of those whose entire lives are motivated by love. Their daily lives are quiet testaments to love. They join philanthropic groups whose mission is a unified force of selfless love in offering shelter and meals and heat and scholarships—to those they know personally only as fellow human beings in need of love. They brighten their own corner **and** shed their light afar.

When my sister lived her last several months under hospice care, my husband and I drove two hundred miles weekly to sit with her. She was often alone on those long afternoons, and she ached for comforting companionship even though her attention faltered and she dozed. My husband would bring his guitar and sing her favorite songs. We brought in delectable treats and filled her with stories from our own lives. We held her hand and smoothed her brow while her husband busied himself away from the suffering. We loved her particularly but also generally. Her need for the human touch was clear. And at her funeral my husband felt her need profoundly. He remembered Jesus's admonition to give your coat to one requiring the warmth of care and laid his own jacket in the grave for her. Selfless love sustains us even in death. It is indeed twice-blessed.

LOVING EXERCISES

1. Think of a loving act you might perform that no one will know was done by you. Now do it. Capture in your journal how this makes you feel.

2. Write a detailed portrait of someone you admire who exhibits selfless love. Go over it again, edit it, and make it better. Then give the person a copy.

3. In what ways can you show love in your community? In what ways might you improve your local circumstances for everyone?

LOVE OF ENVIRONMENT

"Love does not dominate; it cultivates."
— Johann Wolfgang von Goethe

"Loving people live in a loving world. Hostile people
live in a hostile world. Same world."
— Wayne Dyer

I knew a man, a college president, who was of
Scottish descent. His speaking style was folksy, and
he loved to pepper a conversation with personal
anecdotes. He often shared a life motto passed on to
him by his father: "Laddie," he'd relate, "always
leave a place better than you found it." Humans by
basic nature seem to have an instinct for
improvement of our environs. We might even go so
far as to call this a desire for order. Cinema offers us
countless visions of a couple or even a single
individual who, in a post-apocalyptic world, in total
solitude, sets out to "civilize" their space. They
construct an efficient shelter. They clear the land.
They dam a creek and divert running water through
a sluice toward their dwelling. They dig a well. They

make paths and mark trails through woods. They stack firewood. They clear away rubbish and litter. They sweep their shelter and rake the grounds. And they cultivate a garden.

We might term these survival activities a form of self-care, but they also quickly evolve into a type of love emanating from a sense of unity, a sense of belonging. As a Sioux prayer acknowledges, people and places are part of the same animating love: "Teach us to walk the soft Earth as relatives to all that live." If we pay attention, we become intimately familiar with our surroundings, our space.

When I lived for a year in a house on the edge of the sea, I walked every day, the same path to the beach, the same stretch of sandy shore. Soon I began to clear and improve the rocky path, which at first had seemed to me a vast rubble field. I removed stray stones and stacked them in satisfying pagodas. I monitored the sounds of the surf and noted each new item dropped by the seas onto the beach, my beach. The space and I merged, becoming intimate friends, and I watched out for that place. I internalized the various sounds of the surf and chronicled them in a poem.

SURFSOUND

" I have grown unconscious of the roar,
and though it sounds all day long in my
waking ears, and all night long in my

sleeping ones, my ears seldom send
on the long tumult to the mind."
– Henry Beston

Conch shell held to the ear.
Two jets circling on recon.
Dumptruck run amok.
Murmur of seagods.
Distant herd of bison spooked.
Anticipation whispered in the wind.
A hundred cauldrons coming to a boil.
Army marching by at double time.
Tanks passing on into Prague.
Earth's whole census in a marathon.
Women rinsing laundry in the stream.
Women shaking out straw mattresses.
Cheers of the fans at a World Cup game.
Avalanche.
Clutch of angry vipers.
Iceberg breaking apart.
River at full flood.
The Rip Van Winkle pulling into Grand Central.
All the world's sadists cracking the whip.
Whipped cream spraying on ambrosia.
Termites clearing out a fallen log.
Congregation mouthing the Lord's Prayer.
Distant thunder.
Growl of Cerberus.
Paradiddle of timpani.
Earth's engine at full throttle.
Ovational applause.
Cars on a nearby freeway.
The caissons rolling along.
The earth intoning OM.

The ocean and I became familiars.

In a way where we dwell becomes an extension of our identity, a vital part of who we are. "Where are you from?" we ask a new acquaintance. "Which house do you live in?" Our own character shines forth from our place and our tending of it. From the moment we arrive, we work to make a place our own.

There is an aesthetic of beauty or of satisfying order that often drives our efforts. We establish even and discernible boundaries by building fences and planting hedges. We trim and mow and rake and neaten our environs. Inside, we arrange furnishings and sweep and dust and mop. Part of a self-care regimen works to maintain both order and beauty around us. We improve even the meanest of dwellings by adding a porch or a patio to enhance our occupation of that space. A well-tended property reflects a well-lived life filled with an over-spilling love.

And we share this enhancement of place with other living entities. We hang feeders with hummingbird nectar and bird seeds. We construct birdbaths and toad houses. We attach bat boxes high up on trees. We even plant new, colorful trees. Nothing shows a love for humanity unborn and a trust in the future more than an elderly person planting a tree. As a Greek proverb maintains, "A society grows great when old men plant trees in whose shade they know they shall never sit."

I knew a woman who as part of her yearly routine always planted one hundred daffodil bulbs in autumn, no matter where she was. She left every place better than she found it—in a sea of yellow spring delight that self-propagated season after season. This activity becomes a constant both actually and metaphorically. As Voltaire famously has his philosopher Pangloss remark at the end of *Candide* after extensive world travel, *"Il faut cultiver notre jardin"*: But we must cultivate our garden.

To me, this is a motto filled with love that can guide our daily living. What shall we set out to accomplish in the world? Every small action can be motivated by love, and each begins with a self-care that automatically is extended to others and is reflected in our space and place. An elderly woman who has cleared a parcel of land and put in squash seeds saved from zucchini given to her by a friend makes a tidy and productive showing of ordered mounds in front of her home—and then, of course, shares her autumn bounty with all her friends and neighbors. Much wonder and magic can come from staying put. Such simple activities become paradigms of love, and they are sustaining all 'round. Acts of love are self-renewing and always give an at least twice-blessed return on the investment.

If we become infirm or weakened by age, love of our space can often sustain our activity. One can always—albeit slowly, yet deliberately—tend a garden. In this task too dwells a satisfying sense of intimacy. The garden becomes a reflection of who we are, and it embodies a history—of decisions we have made, of vicissitudes of local weather and seasons, of our successes and failures, of plants fostered and others purged. The mind automatically makes these connections, which we can bolster through careful attention and even documentation, as in a journal.

"Last year the bleeding heart was in bloom by now," we remember, and we rush to examine it in its place. Sure enough, its reddish stems have pushed up boldly from the ground and leaves and hearts are forming. The intrepid return of perennials places our own life into a temporal context, and if we tend to that garden, we are simultaneously both magnified and infolded as an equal into its processes.

Poet Robert Aitken captures this intimate connection:

> Watching gardeners label their plants
> I vow with all beings
> to practice the old horticulture
> and let the plants identify me.

The garden relies on us to be what it is, yet it will persist without us. As Thomas Jefferson famously noted, "Tho' an old man, I am but a young gardener." Life loves to be. It finds a way, renewing all that participate in its perennial process.

We might call this urge to in-dwell and cultivate a harmonious place the Edenic impulse. The rise of the metropolis has separated us from a grounding in spaces we might dignify and distinguish by our own character. We live corporately in efficient and uniform units. We travel to hotels and resorts remarkable primarily for their sameness, plunked down anywhere with little sense of the integrity of people in a place. Yet the spirit of love begins inevitably to make an appearance.

Travelers are fascinated by witnessing dwellings of ancestors long-gone. We are drawn to places like Pompeii, a city clearly still infused by the love of its millennial inhabitants. We add our personalized loving improvements to barn houses, carriage houses, mews houses, oast houses, yurts, stone cottages, igloos, craftsman homes, Victorian mansions, sod houses—any human space retaining its original sense of an abode enhanced by the love of self-care extended outside itself.

Such activity distinguishes us but also unifies us with humans over time. When we tend to our own welfare by improving our place, by cultivating our garden, we manifest at the most basic level human love. This is a poem I wrote to make connections between small domestic activity and profound love, and it was celebrated by the Oregon Poetry Association as the best poem of the year.

SWEEPING: THREE SCENES

I.

For flagstones find
a primitive straw broom uneven and rough.
On a summer's morning
sprinkle the stones first
as if preparing shirts to iron.
Each stroke scrubs, laves
the flags pristine as a terrazzo
tended by crones in the shadow of Vesuvius.

II.

Indoors a flat-angled broom
works best. An even pull
followed by short-stroked passes
garners surprises—that pin
that dropped mixed in with crumbs
and the fine underfur of the cat.
My mother swept each evening
when dishes were done, her final chore,
a clean floor primed for next morning.

III.

My husband sweeps in the nude,

sometimes in just a shirt.
He hums while he sweeps,
careful to reach each corner,
his passes deliberate and slow.
This is his way to make love,
centering first like a pot on the wheel
then clearing a path
for the day to proceed as it will.

Much-loved poet Mary Oliver reveals a similar philosophy in her poem called "My Work is Loving the World":

My work is loving the world.
Here the sunflowers, there the hummingbird -
equal seekers of sweetness.
Here the quickening yeast; there the blue plums.
Here the clam deep in the speckled sand.

Are my boots old? Is my coat torn?
Am I no longer young and still not half-perfect? Let me
keep my mind on what matters,
which is my work,
which is mostly standing still and learning to be
astonished.
The phoebe, the delphinium.
The sheep in the pasture, and the pasture.
Which is mostly rejoicing, since all ingredients are
here,

Which is gratitude, to be given a mind and a heart
and these body-clothes,
a mouth with which to give shouts of joy
to the moth and the wren, to the sleepy dug-up clam,

telling them all, over and over, how it is
that we live forever.

Pay close attention; accept yourself however you are;
be patient enough to be still in nature and learn "to be
astonished"; practice gratitude; and remember the
spark of being that joins us all and renders us
immortal.

LOVING EXERCISES

1. Think of planting and tending a garden as a metaphor for you as you make the space you inhabit your own. What activity do you consider to be "your garden," and what words would you use to describe it? Seek out a community garden and become a member who tends to it regularly.

2. Remember a place you have lived and recall ways in which you left it better than you found it.

3. Consider which area of a home best illustrates the love of the person who lives there. How do you express love in your own dwelling?

LIVING IN GRATITUDE

"Just to be is a blessing. Just to live is holy."
—Rabbi Abraham Heschel

A most-loved Biblical scripture is the 23d Psalm of David. In the King James Version translation we find the verse to offer a soothing incantation asserting a message of assurance and gratitude, almost like a mantra. For decades I have repeated this psalm mentally each night as I lie in bed. The poetry falls into a pattern echoing the comfort of a human heartbeat:

Yea' though I walk' through the val' ley
of the shad' ow of death' ...

Lubba dub lubba dub lubba dub. The comfort of this rhythm is primal and parental. Metaphorically I feel it as the heartbeat of our creator, living within me and animating my own alive-ness. Instantly I am calmed, as if hearing my own mother's heartbeat.

With the prospect of certain death, for we are all mortal, what love sustains us in life? The psalm continues and elaborates with stunning simplicity. First is the love of the creative force, which we carry within and which animates our being: we shall not want. Second is the concept of loving self-care; we are nourished in green pastures, protected along the still waters, which run dangerously deep. Third, recognizing the creator at work within us is our mandate and its own reward: we walk the paths of righteousness *for his name's sake*. Fourth is a social aspect of belonging to a certain tribe or family, which prospers safely even in the face of enemies and adversity—the cruel world out there. A comforting force of belonging to the family of humanity protects and guides us: thy rod and thy staff, which are the tools of the shepherd to lay a comforting touch on the shoulders of sheep within the herd, who prefer the huddle, the press of kinship and togetherness.

This perfect prayer of gratitude ends with a confident assertion. With such kinds of love firmly in place, what must inevitably come?

Good' ness and mer' cy shall fol' low me
all' the days' of my life',
and I shall dwell' in the house'
of the lord' forev' er.

Lubba dub lubba dub lubba dub. We are grateful for another day. We are grateful to be alive. We are grateful for sustenance and safety. We are grateful for family and friends. These are the basics of love. We do well to recognize and acknowledge them routinely. As Chief Tecumseh said of "the joy of living," "If you see no reason for giving thanks, the fault lies in yourself." Such prayers remind us to see our blessings and live in daily gratitude.

To bear a sense of gratitude is to face each day with hope and with a kindness toward our fellow travelers, the Golden Rule in action. As Wayne Dyer notes, the identical universe houses both the optimist and the pessimist, the Pollyanna and the cynic, those who wear rose-colored glasses and those who don dark shades. As we perceive and interact with the world, we fashion and affect its reality for ourselves. The Golden Rule implies that we might expect from others the same kind of loving concern we ourselves exhibit. We can model through our own emotions-become-actions the world **as we'd like it to be.**

To project the aura of gratitude—to allow gratitude to define and guide our actions—defies our western model of aggressive selfhood and life as a competition with others, whom we must vie against, defeat, destroy, or beat into submission. Countless bumper stickers extol being "in the lead," having "all the toys," "winning" at sports or politics, taunting others to "eat my dust." Living in a state of gratitude requires us to rethink the paradigms that guide our social interactions, as co-operative rather than competitive, as being rather than having.

Gratitude almost inevitably leads us into empathy, which is, of course, the foundation of the Golden Rule. We must use our own sense of goodness and well-being for ourselves as a measure of our treatment of everyone else.

How do we feel when someone curses us or calls us a derogatory name? Demeaned, valueless—and generally terrible. Why would we inflict that feeling on someone else? How do we feel when someone cuts us off in traffic and flips us an obscene gesture? Annoyed at best—further, perhaps helpless and endangered. Why would we try to frighten a fellow driver who might then move on to harm others? How do we feel when someone cheats us in a business transaction, willfully scams us, or, to escalate the pattern, breaks into our house, robs us, mugs us, or steals our identity? Violated in our basic human rights—disrespected and diminished.

The person who desires to demean, frighten, endanger, cheat, disrespect, or diminish others as a way of life forgets that we are co-members of the family of humankind, brothers and sisters rather than individuals alone. And, in a kind of karmic justice, such a person may discover similar treatment in return. We participate in creating the world we inhabit: as we sow, so shall we reap. A current saying urges us to "Practice random acts of kindness."

Such selfless acts heedless of instant reward create ripple effects, like a stone tossed into a lake, and they are always twice-blessed. When the return for a loving action seems deferred or delayed, we must not abandon a loving way of life. A five-hundred-year-old proverb proposes we might "kill others with kindness"—a form of gentle "warfare" that wins over adversaries rather than conquering them.

While societies formulate laws to prohibit criminal actions and regulate civic interaction, we have less formal, generally unwritten yet agreed upon mores to guide ordinary daily social activity. Everyone notices and becomes affected when these begin to break down. We must respond to rudeness, slights, insults, unruliness, bullying, taunting, coarse language, and even assault on occasion. Age-old scripture advises that we "turn the other cheek," specifically the left cheek, which is regularly misread as a passive invitation for further abuse.

Paul T. Penley explains, rather, that the action refers directly to how Roman soldiers struck Jews in the face. If they hit with the right hand in a demeaning back-hand slap, it hit the right cheek, but a blow in anger toward an equal landed on the left cheek. Truly, then, we can interpret the metaphor as an invitation to confident integrity: maintaining calmness and dignity in the face of chaos and violation. We refuse to engage in demeaning interaction or to be brought down to low-level response. We model respect of others in our own actions—and re-actions. We turn the left cheek.

Perhaps no area of interaction offers an opportunity for kindness, respect, and empathy so immediately and clearly as conversation. We reveal much of our own loving character in speaking with others. Some people seem to be waiting for an opening so they can just tell their own story, hear their own voice. They "listen" only to pick up the topic and get ready to chime in about themselves. Often this seems like a form of verbal warfare, as it is simple self-assertion above all else. They do not respond in conversation, and there is no forward movement, no give and take. By passing over the other's statement to take control of the conversation they essentially erase the other person as of no matter. And likely no memory will remain of their encounters, for they do not take in, register, or process the other's communication. They are mere clanging cymbals.

So many chances for a loving connection can be lost with this pattern. One may relate an incident or a feeling as a form of self-revelation—implicitly asking for advice, sympathy, or consolation—really a validation of being. We open ourselves up. We hope to be truly listened to and truly heard. "I hear you," we say. I understand. I acknowledge you. I am grateful for our connection.

Genuine listening requires patience, practice, and restraint. A thoughtful response enfolds the statement of the other person in a loving concern. "Tell me more about that," we might encourage. Or "That must have been a joyful event for you" we might offer as endorsement. Restatement of what we heard is always a strong affirmation of loving listening.

We can discover gratitude in conversation with those who trust us with their own humanity. To listen with empathy is to "feel into" another's experience and thus to enhance our own sense of the human experience. Listening well is twice-blessed. When we share another's humanity, we augment our own experience and multiply our reasons for gratitude.

When we truly live each day with the heartbeat of gratitude resonating our very being, every action spreads this gratitude to others. Recently when I was in a parking lot walking toward a store, a gust of wind took a woman's hat and raced it away. Instinctively, full of gratitude for my own agility such as it is and empathy for her consternation, I chased the hat down and retrieved it for her.

I expected no return. We were in this together, and this was an act of kindness that seemed ordinary and necessary to me. Yet her response filled the space between us with much more than I had invested. It was clear that she was moved that a stranger cared and acted without hesitation. It was clear that she felt valued and cared for, by a loving sister of the family of humankind. Gratitude leavens our human connection. When it inevitably permeates our actions, it grows and rises, like yeasted bread. And like daily bread, it nourishes and sustains our being.

This may even be the implicit mandate of our creator. "I didn't ask to be born," the childish say in anger or frustration. Others through the ages ponder the meaning of life, wondering what philosophical truths should guide their choices. What is the right path for us? What are we obliged to do with the gift of living?

The best choice is simple: fully be. "Be here now," the Buddhists advise us. Giving credence to love as the creative force of the cosmos, tending with love to our own self-care, filling our hearts with gratitude that results in loving action—this sequence leads us to our imperative. If we fail to become as fully human as we can, we betray this brief span of the miracle of our time on earth as creatures with bodies and souls.

It seems not by coincidence that Taoists view life as a "way": the Tao is "a person on a path." In all religious philosophies we try to approach the truth of the matter in allusive metaphors. A path implies a journey; it is a way, a direction, with forward movement. Each day, each action, comprises a part of the whole, and all the segments add up to the totality of our life: where (and how) we end up. What will we have gained? And what will we have given, to have our life make a difference?

Whether or not we concur or acquiesce, each step is forward. We progress in spite of ourselves. Yet each moment, each step, is at once discrete as well as part of the whole journey. So we are constantly affirming our existence and the love that created us and animates and guides us. If we energize each step with gratitude for being, we begin to fulfill our mandate. "Just to be is a blessing. Just to live is holy."

LOVING EXERCISES

1. Whether or not you believe in a creator, articulating thanks for good fortune is important. Count your blessings, no matter how small. Devise a prayer of gratitude and write it down. Recite it to yourself upon waking and prior to sleeping. Try to synchronize your words with the rhythm of your heartbeat. Notice the calmness come over you along with a positive change in attitude.

2. The next time you have an in-person conversation with someone, consciously try to engage in patient listening. Try to respond heartfully to each of their statements without taking control. Reach out and touch their hand. Afterwards, think about how you felt during that time together.

3. Using your imagination and creative skills, draw a chart of your life path. Decide on the map's parameters and objectively indicate highs and lows, direct routes and diversions. Where shall the path lead in the future?

LETTING GO, LETTING BE

"The most important thing in life is to learn how to give out love, and to let it come in."—Morrie Schwartz

"Don't brood. Get on with living and loving. You don't have forever."—Leo Buscaglia

Both my mother and my father kept a daily diary. In my teenage years I was critical of their entries, which focused on chronicling events and activities. Theirs was a generation that did not freely express or share their deepest feelings, made clear to me in a heart-wrenching sentence my dad wrote, "Found out today I have cancer," with no commentary on that fact. And not long after that, the cancer took his life.

Mother always noted the day's temperature in her five-year diary, perhaps because she grew up in farmlands where weather was vital for human prosperity. I had a friend who kept more of a journal rather than a diary, and she wrote daily, profusely, about the ups and downs of her emotions. This was at the other end of the spectrum.

At various times of my life I've tried journal writing. As a teenager I had a small book with a wee lock and key. I'm glad I can't locate it now. I'm sure I noted what I wore and what boy talked to me at school. How embarrassing, and how ephemeral. In my twenties I took a five-week self-guided jaunt through Europe, and I attempted to capture each day's experiences and sights without comment, pure sensory description, for the art and architecture were overwhelming, like romantic dreams come true, like books and history and historic figures brought to life.

Sometimes I stumble across these notes jotted on cards in a folding case and relive the joy of that young woman discovering the world. Her description of seeking refuge from a sudden downpour in Florence's Il Duomo, only to discover a solo cellist playing Bach in the basilica brings back that magical event with vividness. And her amazement at walking up the steps of Canterbury Cathedral, which she found dented in, worn down by hundreds of years of feet, makes my heart beat more quickly even today.

Later, when after a nearly twenty-year marriage I felt the relationship, plagued by illnesses and career conflicts, begin to break down, I broached another journal. I bought a handsome leather-bound volume with blank pages—but the pressure of the formality of that book weighed me down. I wrote in perfect printing, trying to make no errors or false starts. I carefully crafted the content and style of each entry as if I were producing a literary masterpiece. I guess I thought someone would discover it some day after I was a dead famous author, so it was not genuine. Too aware of what a reader might think, the writing was formal and devised for others rather than for myself.

We all need to find a ritualized way to establish an acceptable narrative of our lives. While we also strive to "be here now" and live fully in the moment, our personal story includes causes and effects, good and poor choices, vicissitudes of fate and chance, unexpected strokes of luck and serendipity. It is helpful to see where we've been and what designs our patterns may trace, as choices we make now help to determine where the path leads next. Like Aeneas leaving the burning Troy carrying his father on his back and leading his son by the hand, we live at once here and now while carrying our past into the future. This is the human paradox defined by living consciously in time. Writing down how we perceive our life story is one way to see the path clearly. Days will go by whether or not we plan and note them. We are obliged to participate fully to understand our "way."

But journaling is only one of several alternatives. If we are fortunate, we may have children or grandchildren with whom to discuss how things came to be. "Tell me about the time you . . ." a young family member may ask, and stories are taken to heart, becoming part of their history too. Some of us have life-long friends who may even share earlier memories, and we can talk things out to gain a new perspective. I have cherished friends, some for fifty years, who have been sounding boards and reality checks, helping shape my own sense of my self and my life.

Setting aside a time for regular quiet meditation may work for some of us. We may create mental scenarios—sort of like a life movie—that reveal cause and effect between events in time and enhance self-understanding. Working with a counselor can also be helpful. The best of these therapists prompt us into thoughtful storytelling, connecting the dots of our own life events by perceiving them, articulating them, and placing them into patterns. Therapy, "the talking cure," works to help us fashion an acceptable narrative of our lives.

Whichever method we choose for self-reflection, we will discover that our story is fluid and the outcome open for interpretation. Like a literary narrative, it may "mean" several things at once depending on our approach. Our memory may in fact block out parts of events we find detrimental to the story we want to live. Or in a retelling we may sculpt a sequence so that we serve as victim—or perhaps, on the other hand, the hero of our own lives as Charles Dickens said. The same story might lead in many directions, like Jorge Borges' garden of forking paths.

Through memory, self-scrutiny, and reflection, we continually make choices to create the kind of story we want our life to be. Each of us has made mistakes in the past. To be human, to live, is sometimes to make a wrong move. Will we allow these mis-steps to dominate our story? Or through reflection, will we move toward a happier ending?

The choice belongs to each of us. I have an acquaintance whose constant topic of conversation, over decades, has been how she could have been greatly successful if only. . . . The "if only" changes— if only a certain person hadn't blocked her or been biased against her, if only she had better health, if only luck worked in her favor. The fault, and the responsibility, for outcomes, perhaps changes for the better, is never hers. Cassius in Shakespeare's "Julius Caesar" knew this error in thinking well: "The fault, dear Brutus, lies not in the stars, but in ourselves. . . ."

Once we become participants in understanding and in fact shaping our life patterns and future paths, we can live in society mindfully. We all know people who seem constantly flustered and frustrated as they allow urgencies of each day to direct their motions and attention. No time to eat, no time to exercise, no time to talk, no time to relax, no time to think or to ponder. They flit from demand to demand, relinquishing control over and awareness of their passing time. As we become mindful of how we live—and how it all adds up to a meaning for us—calmness and serenity settle upon us. We are better able to handle and process adversity and setbacks. And with a calm acceptance of our own life path, we are able to extend ourselves with a genuine sense of emotional empathy for others.

This is the true benefit of self-aware and mindful living. As we understand and contextualize our own life events, we become able to forgive others who have been players in our own stories—and then others whose narratives we now encounter. We come to feel little need to bend others to our sense of plot or to reject other paths. We may in fact relish and enjoy difference without feeling a threat to our own selfhood.

One source of anger and misunderstanding occurs when we try to script others' lives and characters for them, appropriating their story. We torture ourselves when they don't act according to our expectations, our plans for their life. As my niece once explained to my sister, "Mom, I'm not YOU!" To forgive others is to allow them their own autonomous narrative, and it releases us to love.

86

Keeping in mind the wisdom of the Golden Rule, we may decide to assume that most people do not intend the ill effects on others they may sometimes cause. While it may not be an infallible assumption, this state of mind can help liberate our own sense of insult, resentment, or indignation—all part of letting go and letting be.

Constantly reliving past slights keeps us from being here now and moving on. Rehearsing resentments in our minds keeps those wrongs vividly alive for us. But understanding the past can help us walk our path now with a sense of informed liberation. As we forgive others who have—purposely or not—harmed us, we can also forgive ourselves for past mistakes, past patterns, portions of our story we learn from and let be at rest.

Rather than seeking a temporary sense of oblivion through alcohol, drugs, or glutting ourselves with rich and filling foods, we would better try to clear the mind of distractions through a self-aware meditative process, whichever one we might choose. We will always carry our past along with us. How much happier we can be if we confront those events that disturb us and put them mentally in an understandable context. Seeing our own mistakes and calling them out is part of self-forgiveness, and it makes us even more fully human. The days WILL pass whether we participate or not. Better to continue on our path with an enhanced sense of humility. Let go, and let be—to fully be here now.

LOVING EXERCISES

1. If you don't already keep a diary or journal, get one going now. Set aside a regular time for a daily entry. Note down your activities and accomplishments, your thoughts and feelings. Especially note milestones or achievement of goals. In a year, read over the sequence. Does it have a plot?

2. Think of a long-time grudge that you've nursed. Re-experience fully but now with mindfulness what your feelings were that resulted in anger and resentment. Then consciously calm those feelings by trying to see the other person's situation. With this new perspective, let go of your grudge.

3. What do you consider to be the biggest mistake you ever made in your life choices? Think about the context and conditions surrounding that choice. What were your other options and where would they have led? Perhaps you did the best you could at that moment, in those circumstances. Forgive yourself.

EACH DAY A CHANCE TO LOVE

"If there is a day to act on the Love in your soul it is today, it is this moment."—Mike Dolan

"She loves you, yeah, yeah, yeah," the Beatles sing joyfully, and to be loved is entirely self-affirming indeed. We walk on air; we glow with a special aura. But being loved also inspires loving, and that is its wonder. When we feel loved, we spread it around, enfolding others in the embrace of oneness we're experiencing. From being beloved, we become lovers, those who love. And this may be the fullest expression of that spark that animates us—"for God so loved the world. . . ." When we love, we share our portion of the great creative force informing the universe.

91

Scriptures realize that they must use the given word, LOVE, to approach this phenomenon, but, finding it limited and ultimately inadequate, they move to metaphor. We are urged, for instance, to let our light shine rather than hiding it under a barrel, or to light a candle rather than cursing the darkness. Our "light" is the creative force of love within ourselves. These metaphors are visual analogies for loving, for expressing the self through loving action. A most-cherished text is in the Bible's letter from Paul to the Corinthians, chapter 1:13, where he tries to express and capture the centrality of love:

Love is patient and kind;
love does not envy or boast;
it is not arrogant or rude.
It does not insist on its own way;
it is not irritable or resentful;
it does not rejoice at wrongdoing,
but rejoices with the truth.
Love bears all things, believes all things,
hopes all things, endures all things.
Love never ends. . . .
So now faith, hope, and love abide,
these three;
but the greatest of these is love.

Clearly, Paul reveals here that love can be a guiding force in both personal and community life. While we may feel that we love best when we are beloved, this larger sense of *caritas* comes from within each of us. Once we acknowledge that we are animated by the spirit of love, we experience its effect as rays of light sent out into our world or as ripples in water radiating from the love that awakens our actions.

We rise in the morning filled with the creative force; we exercise the self-care rituals that honor that love; and this prepares us for a day of loving action, each and every day. Rather than dreaming of some grand heroics from our lives, we may discover in these small, habitual, and regular patterns of love the fullest way to make an effect on the world. Love. Simply love. Loving action is sure to follow.

Popular music and movies have trained us to think about love as something that happens to the young. Within these patterns "finding" love is the focus, and after that everything is well set up for life—or it falls apart tragically, the death of love. Some of my favorite films work this way: in the comedic "Man Up," Simon Pegg portrays a man who approaches a woman in a train station whom he erroneously thinks is his blind date. So surprised is she that she plays along, and after really hitting it off with him finally reveals the error. He becomes angry and they experience tenseness, then sorrow, but realize they have fallen deeply in love and of course eventually overcome all obstacles.

Or, on the other extreme, in the well-loved classic "An Affair to Remember," Deborah Kerr and Cary

Grant have a madcap fling aboard an ocean liner. They separate for six months to get their lives in order so they can be together, and they are to meet on an appointed day and time on the rooftop of the Empire State Building. As he waits up there for her, he hears the sirens, unaware that she has been struck by a car while rushing to keep their date. He is dashed, and she is debilitated, embarrassed after healing to contact him in her altered condition. So they live sadly apart—until he finds her by serendipity and rushes in to her daybed to love her still—and again. We sigh just hearing these plots—age-old patterns of love found, love threatened or lost, love regained after all.

If, in our own lives, we are fortunate enough to experience some version of these plots, we must nourish the romantic love we find and realize our good fortune. Nothing so opens our hearts as romantic love, and nothing so devastates us when it is lost. And we must know that it is not the sole element to set us up for the good life. Sometimes we see couples who so take one another for granted that they no longer exercise even the ordinary kindness and polite respect they endow upon strangers. At the other extreme, we find those who have made a small self-contained universe of their love, closing out contact and interaction beyond themselves.

Even with a strong and secure romantic anchor to our lives, we need to find outlets to extend our *caritas* beyond this center. Like John Milton's comment on virtue, a cloistered love is untested, incomplete. The best circumstance enables us to live our love, in the world as at home, on a daily basis. Love itself is neither monolithic nor one-dimensional, and it will, like a protozoan, adapt and change over time. A single love may deepen; a love undergoing trials may develop scars and new paths for expressing that developed and evolved love.

Love is always changing and always the same. And love will out. As we love and care for ourselves, as we develop strong familial and romantic bonds, we will naturally extend our love as an informing and powerful force into our daily activities. One who truly knows love will show that love to the world.

Once our youth is long past, we do not become bereft of love. On the contrary, time nurtures in us a vigorous, enhanced opportunity for showing and sharing love. The elderly may, having lost the romantic connections of their young days and middle life, like giggling and naïve teenagers discover romantic love again. But even those who live alone can exercise their love every day. Our experiences of loving through time hone and burnish our capacities. We no doubt have loved and lost—many of us again and again. Love has a self-renewing resilience that lends to the lover patience and equanimity. Those who live by love find those opportunities for giving, sharing, teaching, supporting, helping, nourishing, and offering profound loving kindness to those in need.

When my own husband died, I sought help for healing in a hospital-sponsored grief group. Here those of us bereft of someone we loved worked through our sadness, came to terms with loss and mortality, offered support to those in the same state, and learned how to go on. One lesson was not to think love is dead, not to give up on ourselves or on love.

One group member was a woman twenty years my senior who seemed especially devastated at the loss of her partner, and she had spent the prior few months, since his passing, producing a volume of poems she called "The Year with No Summer." She and I have since become great friends in part because, in the midst of her own grief, in a broad act of love, she freely gave copies of this book to everyone she met. Even though her own life was altered by a profound loss of love, she began to rebuild connections through a loving act of reaching out and offering her solace by sharing her own sorrow.

To isolate ourselves is an act counter to the creative force of love within us. Like interest on an investment or a certificate of deposit, love given, love bestowed, always accumulates our own store. It is always twice-blessed. Those of us who sometimes feel we are living empty lives devoid of meaning, a daily drudge of work we dislike, struggles with traffic jams, conflicts with rude or unthinking strangers, and a deep physical exhaustion accompanied by a spirit longing for some fulfillment, might discover a remedy in reaching out in acts of love.

The miracle of this cure is felt immediately, and it continues to accrue. Rather than trying to fill our void with mindless consumption—another concert, another basketball game, another drink, more recreational drugs, a crowded flight to a crowded resort on a "paradise" island, or the ultimate version of "death by chocolate" cake—we will find a better panacea in acting out with love. Ironically, giving fills the empty space inside that no consumption or acquisition can reach, and it reveals the "why" of being human. Loving fulfills who we are.

How many of us know someone who seems stuck in a teenage mindset and lifestyle even into their fifties and beyond? Often deeply self-centered, these people seem to marry for the wrong reasons—propinquity, having "good times," superficial physical attraction—all without love. When the marriage fails, as it inevitably will, they quickly search for the same again, a companion who may enjoy partying and pursuing leisure activities all while avoiding inner knowledge or achieving the ability to give of themselves in love.

Even when these people think they "have it all," they feel lost and empty. There is a sort of franticness in their quest for pre-determined activities plotted to offer the forms of fulfillment— without the content. Without empathy the self shrivels rather than thrives. Without actual love, such lives are tragic losses. If at times we find a modern sense of despair overcoming us, we should consciously try to cultivate fellow feeling for those we encounter each day. Maybe we feel that friends and family are not as attentive as we would like or that we are taken for granted—at work, or at home. The medicine for despair is to reach out in acts of love.

Sometimes I try to visualize my heart having the capacity to enfold others in a grand embrace of love, simply human to human. Even on those days when I feel self-absorbed or self-pitying, this releases a curative force within. To get out of oneself ironically enhances and fulfills the self.

In this way our actions in the world can affect and even alter our outlook and feelings of self-worth. Molecule by molecule, atom by atom, our bodies react to the power of loving. This, in fact, is the lesson of meditative exercise—t'ai chi, yoga, or simply serene, conscious, meditative breathing. By centering our mind on the inflow and outflow of breath, which embodies the spirit of living, we both calm and activate who we are—and our capacity to reach out in love.

Stimulated by the unifying power of body-mind-spirit, we vibrate with loving potential. And then each and every day becomes another chance to love. A life lived day by day through finding opportunities for loving is like a cup that runneth over. We become filled and overflowing with the power of loving.

LOVING EXERCISES

1. Consciously perform a loving action that you know will never be rewarded, and tell no one else about it. Find your candidate for loving by using empathy. Who, at this moment, needs your love?

2. Consider in depth how you behave when you're feeling low or depressed. How can you balance self-care with loving at large? Try reaching out to a neighbor or finding a younger person you can mentor in a particular activity. Volunteer to take a child on a brief fun trip to a park or a museum.

3. If you habitually turn to food, cigarettes, alcohol, or drugs for comfort and solace, try to pinpoint exactly how you're feeling when you have such a "need." When you get this urge for over-indulgence or oblivion, try reaching out to an elderly friend or relative. Listen to what's going on in their heart and offer the genuine love of your caring presence to experience a new kind of "high."

LOVE IN THE TIME OF CORONAVIRUS

"The only regret I will have in dying is if it is not for love."—Gabriel García Márquez, *Love in the Time of Cholera*

"What if religion was each other? If our practice was our life? If prayer was our words? What if the temple was the Earth? If forests were our church? If holy water - the rivers, lakes, and oceans? What if meditation was our relationships? If the Teacher was life? If wisdom was knowledge? If love was the center of our being."—Ganga White

In a mere few weeks across the globe everyone's lifestyle changed. Americans had experienced for the most part three decades of unprecedented expectations for the present and the future. While we still faced social problems of inequity, our long-standing challenge of America as the great

101

experiment, the large portion of us were free from immediate life-threatening disease, traveled wherever we wanted to go, and sought pleasurable entertainment. When we had a glitch or a setback, it was a "first world" problem. Most of us could communicate instantly, consult endless information on the internet, buy what we wanted there and elsewhere, frequent restaurants, drive luxurious and enormous cars, drink fancy drinks and take fancy recreational drugs, and fly from coast to coast or island hop as we pleased. We could seek glamorous, exciting entertainment like professional sports, crowded arena concerts, and theme parks. Life was good, full of idle fun and diversion.

Then a minuscule life-form, in pursuing its own robust existence, found the accommodating human host. And it was highly contagious, jumping from host to host by means of airborne droplets. Those of us whose daily lives necessitated group interaction became stymied. Some of us lost our jobs, as these required intense human contact. Children stayed home from school to remain safe. Others were able to work via technology from home. Video conferencing applications and programs boomed. People-loving humans now had to avoid contact with others. Each of us could be a host for murder; each of us could infect loved ones or strangers or inadvertently, casually, become infected ourselves and suffer horribly, perhaps quickly die.

At first we feared for each of us individually. To contract the virus seemed to mean we'd be instantly put on a ventilator and maybe never return from ICU. We began to wear masks, but, it slowly became clear, not so much to protect ourselves as to keep the infection from spreading to others. The coronavirus was forcing each of us to be socially responsible in an era of unprecedented individual freedoms.

Some resisted taking precautions to safeguard their community, in a kind of misguided political statement. No one will tell ME what to do! Some, trusting solely in their own personal experience as the measure of truth, doubted the virulence or even the existence of COVID-19, not personally knowing someone who was infected, who was suffering, who would be forever changed or perhaps not survive at all. The call went out from concerned governmental leaders for us to work together, everyone changing how they moved through their daily activities. We were to think of our neighbor first, ironically by staying apart—keeping our distance, interacting through physical barriers and shields, washing down things we might have mutually touched, checking on the elderly or infirm.

These kinds of public health measures or citizen response in a time of national emergency were not unprecedented. One hundred years ago Americans had universally donned masks during the Spanish flu epidemic; we saw photos of entire families, including the pet cat, in masks. During World War II Americans had answered the call to plant Victory Gardens. During the height of the AIDs epidemic we learned to use condoms with regularity. And in London, all lights were doused during German air raids to help save lives and the city. Citizens working together are a profound force for the common good, historically.

In contrast to people insisting on personal freedoms even if those damaged the public welfare, others without a second thought stepped forward with social conscience in extraordinary acts of heroic citizenship. It goes without saying that health care providers lived up to their professional oaths to "serve humanity—caring for the sick, promoting good health, and alleviating pain and suffering" and beyond, risking their own lives hour by long hour, minute by minute in every encounter. Those who work behind the scenes too gave rigorously, often thanklessly—the cleaners, the food workers, the grocery suppliers, the truckers, those who continued to staff jobs at plants and factories under possibly hazardous conditions. Without even a slight hesitation, service clubs volunteered to prepare and serve meals to community members out of work. Police and emergency personnel offered prescription pick-up and delivery to those more vulnerable to infection.

For all of us the virus forced us into a philosophical moment. Each of us now must assess our odds and make the choices, all day, every day. Do we enjoy eating food at a restaurant (enough to risk infection)? Must we socialize over drinks at a bar or dance club (enough to risk infection)? Need our worship be in a crowded church, or must we keep on with our choir (enough to risk infection)? Can we chance getting a haircut or a pedicure or a tattoo (important enough to risk infection)? Should we go ahead with the holiday family reunion barbecue party of thirty people, young and old (enough to risk infection)? What about the whole clan taking a cake to Aunt Sally for her birthday (important enough to risk infection)? Do we have to put off our vacation at a crowded beach (important enough to risk infection)? Should we refrain from hugging our friends (important enough to risk infection)? What about funeral services for an infected friend who did not survive?

All social aspects of our lives have changed indeed—our routines disrupted—and each of us must be mindful to establish a hierarchy of priorities. We protect ourselves. But we must equally be concerned about our neighbors, and for this we acknowledge kinship in the family of humankind. We acknowledge that we are "our brother's keeper." We accept responsibility that our own actions do not endanger others. As Dr. Anthony

Fauci, the nation's foremost epidemiologist, has said, "I don't know how to explain that you ought to care for others." There is no humane alternative. Loving each other is a given, the *a priori* assumption, the basis from which we then proceed. Now, as in past times of national crisis, we must see ourselves as part of a collective, local, national, global, the family of mankind. We must love our neighbor as ourselves.

Through much of our lives our religious faith or life philosophy is not challenged by direct circumstances. It rests comfortably in the back of our mind, our spirit, as a gentle director of our intentions, and we follow its guidance *more or less*. The pandemic forces a test of our life principles—as individuals and as a community—and requires us to reaffirm them in action.

A friend of mine needed to visit the ER on a non-virus matter during the heat of an outbreak. The hospital staff seemed so careful, to the point of hopeless fear, that she began to consider, "Ah, what if I get the virus here and never go home? I might die!" And of course, this we all know. It is the paradox of living in time that we move ever closer to death from the moment of our birth. As playwright Samuel Beckett visualizes it, humans "give birth astride the grave." Yet we live each day as if death will come for us some time much later. Not today.

This pandemic urgency, an imminent fear of our own death, can bring us to an unprecedented moment of clarity. Our single and sole life appears to us in context and in a continuum. "No man is an island," Dean John Donne observes. "Every man's death diminishes me." Now, at this most precarious of moments, we must care for ourselves AND for others. We become most fully ourselves, living up to our best potential, when we experience and express that inevitable and inviolable kinship. We are all connected.

The pandemic requires that we shore each other up across our boundaries. As one human goes, so go we all. And the expression of the spark of love within each of us sustains and justifies humanity. No matter our age, our gender, our education, our ethnicity, our job, our political party, our religious belief. Such knowledge and such action, of our kinship, poise as the opposite of a self-absorbed and misguided "What's in it for me?" or "No one's going to tell ME what to do!" As we relinquish self-centeredness, ironically we become most fully human, most fully ourselves. Most fully free.

The urgency of the pandemic leads us to the basics of living collectively as human beings. Sometimes it takes a crisis to elicit the best from us. Sometimes it takes a crisis to catalyze change. Despite the luxury with which many of us were living, we have never left behind, as Jesus said, the poor, who will always be with us. We have not solved America's issues of racial injustice. We have not devised, to fulfill Jefferson's dream of an educated citizenry, a universally accessible and effective public school system. With the pandemic, many minimum wage earners are on hiatus. People of color suffer, for myriad reasons, the effect of infection proportionately more than white Americans. And children may risk their own lives or those of their family members to return to school. This is a moment for creative reconfiguring of Americans' obligation to their countryfolk. "Verily I say unto you, Inasmuch as ye have done it unto one of the least of these my brethren, ye have done it unto me," Jesus admonishes us.

Love your neighbor as yourself. We need to strengthen our income safety nets to accommodate a national crisis so that each American can avoid further economic suffering added to fear of infection. Our social conscience should bring us to awareness of the ways in which business as usual has penalized Americans of color—and in light of that awareness be vigilant in our behavior, taking measures toward equality and inclusion and access. And we may seize the opportunity to rethink our schooling, away from seat time to hybrid models of outdoor classes, small group tutoring in cubicles, active hands-on learning modalities, distance learning, and apprenticeship learning. This is the perfect time for a new generation of Sesame Street style video learning clips full of mnemonics and even applications of learning. All can be done with rigorous mask-wearing, proper distancing, and hand-washing with anti-infection cleaning measures in place to protect both the students and those who serve in educational support jobs—not only teachers, but janitors, cafeteria staff, safety personnel, groundsworkers, counselors, office staff. Such an array of community members reveals just how much we are all in this together. We must live carefully, collectively, now, to ensure that we have a future.

Universally, humankind's precepts of individual behavior in society include a Golden Rule: Do unto others as you would have them do unto you. If we have temporarily lost sight of this, we must find it again and make it our beacon, our lodestar. We might look to the thoughts of John Wesley, eighteenth-century founder of Methodism, for sound social philosophy we might still heed and strive for: "I continue to dream [of the time when the potential of] each person can be unleashed. . . .Though we cannot think alike, may we not love alike? May we not be of one heart, though we are not of one opinion? . . . Do with everyone else as you would he should do to you."

Society may be improvable, but it is never "finished." Deviations from what we might conceive as the perfect arrangement and operation are endemic. They come with the territory. But improvement begins with each of us, and it will be continued. That we are not there yet should not stress us unduly. Love begins with each one of us, and there is only the trying.

LOVING EXERCISES

1. Isolate a typical day in your life during the coronavirus. Write down every place you went and every person you had contact with. Did the encounters cause you anxiety? What steps might you take to be more comfortable with our new reality?

2. Select two activities that have been important to your daily life. How might you revisualize these, modify them as necessary, to life under shutdown? Take the specific steps to alter your behavior accordingly.

3. If our lives become permanently altered by a limit to social activity, movement, and interaction, of what can we still be grateful? Make a list of your blessings despite the pandemic.

INVOLVED IN MANKIND: LOVE AND DEATH

"Love is, above all, the gift of oneself." —Jean Anouilh

Somehow the news of fifty lives lost in a mass shooting or someone who jumped off the bridge or a friend whose brother has died of heart disease washes over me without fully sinking in. We know it philosophically: to live means that death will follow. And I take these deaths mostly philosophically. I feel empathy, for young lives cut off, for the despair of a suicide, and for the suffering of those who remain bereft of a member of the family. Yet my own life goes on substantially unchanged.

Until, that is, the people around me, the loved ones in my world, begin to disappear. A friend of mine tells a story about an older woman who responded to my friend's loss of a lover with "Well, you'd better get used to it." In one sense she's right:

113

as we get older we are sure to lose parents, older siblings, friends of our own age who succumb to accidents and diseases, or even our own children by tragic means like car crashes or drug addictions. Yet can we ever "get used to it"? And should we?

This year on my birthday, as my own sister lay in hospice, news came of the death of an old friend. She was seventeen years my senior and I knew she had developed early onset Alzheimer's. For the past twenty years we'd lived separated by a continent. She'd visited here and I'd visited there once or twice; we'd e-mailed; I'd heard news of her from mutual friends; I'd called on her birthday but my message was not returned.

Yet over these twenty years of separation she's been in my mind and in my heart. All that we shared—canoe excursions, sushi dinners with thimble martinis to watch our calories, musical rehearsals and recitals filled with laughter and good harmonies—have stayed with me as a current reality. Another dear friend, a ray of sunshine in her very being, came into my life as an angel when I most needed her. She sat with me as my husband was dying and, over the following years, attended all my readings and lectures and my partner's musical concerts. At one concert she announced that she would be undergoing surgery for a brain tumor. And then, where is the cosmic rationale, where is karma, where is justice? She fell into a coma after surgery and upon regaining consciousness suffered a care-needing existence for nearly three years, then a stroke and a too-soon death. The universe offers us no acceptable logic for such a tragedy. I think a friend with whom we share events and stories of our own past becomes a part of how we live in the world, and in that way part of our own identity, our own being. And their suffering becomes ours as well.

Poet and cleric John Donne famously wrote, "No man is an island entire of itself; every man is a piece of the continent, a part of the main; if a clod be washed away by the sea, Europe is the less; . . . any man's death diminishes me, because I am involved in mankind." The older (and wiser) I become, the more I catch on to the resonance of words I've known for decades. *Each death diminishes me. I am involved in mankind.*

Each life matters. I wish we could remember that we know this. The loss of every life changes the shape of reality. There is a kind of spiritual physics at work in the universe. Our being vibrates through our time on earth, and these ripples move out and affect the others we have dealings with. Everything we affect keeps our imprint and is changed forever, in however small a way.

So when a loved one dies, certainly we feel the immediate hole their non-existence makes. If you've ever seen someone through to death, you know the mystery of that moment. They are here—as the

115

unique and complex miracle every personality is— and then they are no more, as that body.

But the fact of their non-being alters what is now possible for those who remain. We have the responsibility of making sense of the traces they leave, the ripples they have sent into us. We, collectively, bear the conversations, the experiences, the smiles and woes, all that we have shared with them. Their children, their students, their friends, carry pieces of their insight and wisdom, build on these foundations, create grand new testaments to humanity from remnants of the past.

Perhaps it is only through memory that we can understand the impact of those we have lost on who we have become. As we relive our moments with them in memory, the truth of their self shines ever more clearly. The photographs we keep of them on our shelves now seem crystallized and essentialized. In their slightly far-away looks and just the hint of a wise smile, we see pure ivory or ebony polished to a fineness. We refine our understanding of who they were, and in this sense that person continues to evolve.

In a moment of crisis or decision we may remember a single sentence of theirs, or a single act of kindness, of generosity, that will determine our choice of action. We animate their wholeness of being in our own continued existence. We realize them fully by the ways in which they persist in us.

Our sadness is melded into that memory. The departed hover wistfully at the edges of our lives, and we occasionally wonder how they would be now. My father, who seemed worn down at his death at age 62, what would he have been like at 92? And what new guidance might he have given me, as he had so well in the past? I've been left to surmise on my own what he might have told me in those lost years. I've pieced together the traces of his own words, acts, and principles to try to live up to his example. I've carried him on as I walk my own path.

Perhaps we've become inured to the drastic impact of a single person's death. We watch machine gun fire mow down rows of humans in films or task forces try to hew down enemies by any means. In video games we strive to get others in our cross-hairs and annihilate them. These images imprint upon our psyches. We have little compassion for the fallen bodies. We do not feel our humanity. We neglect to remember that *I am involved in mankind.*

While I am neither a politician nor an astute social strategist, I am a human citizen of a global family who can clearly see the horrific absurdity of one country's decision—perhaps one man's decision—to forcibly take over another, usually smaller, independent nation, by obliterating the residents and their places, their dwellings and abodes. Even, or perhaps especially, public figures share an obligation for personal integrity, which has

117

at its base a respect for the lives and welfare of others, to love others as we love ourselves. All-out warfare in the age of nuclear weaponry can only be a self-defeating Armageddon. For . . . temporary material gain . . . political power . . . personal wealth, one achieves a feeble authority over an empty expanse of rubbled land. And that rubble represents the traces of humanity, of our clan of humankind, but no longer the individual lives with their own families, their own pasts, traditions, and plans for the future. Such a war embodies hubris, certainly— what a tragic credit to be linked to one's name—but also universally-held concepts of sin, man against man. It would be well to recall a foundation of being human: *I am involved in mankind. Every death diminishes me.*

I think our new political motto ought to be "Dignify Every Life." Or perhaps we should borrow "No One is an Island" from Dean Donne. All other catchphrases would follow from those—for "greatness" can come only through cherishing the humans who might help achieve it. Recently I read a list of forty-two commandments for living found in the age of Egyptian empire, 1350 BCE, pre-dating Judeaeo-Christian texts. The wisdom in those precepts was remarkably the same as those we know—not to build walls, not to torture or annihilate perceived enemies, not to be covetous or exalt ourselves over others. We are enjoined to "not cause misery . . . not do harm to man . . . not cause the shedding of tears."

Each of us deserves dignity and compassion. Compassion means "to feel with" or "to suffer together." Humanity codified these necessities millennia ago. Let's relearn their necessary truths. *Every life matters more than we can know.* The death of each living person matters to me. *I am involved in mankind.* Each of us is treasured by someone, and every loved one lost changes who we are and alters our world forever.

LOVING EXERCISES

1. Choose someone dear to you whom you have lost through death. Find a photo portrait of that person and display it where you will see it each day. As you peruse their face, think of ways in which they influenced you and what qualities from them you try to emulate.

2. If you find yourself in a group or conversation where there is conflict, how might you serve as a peacemaker? Try to think of verbal strategies to defuse explosive arguments. How might we disagree but still exist harmoniously?

3. If you find yourself envying someone else's possessions, examine what need in yourself this desire stems from. Would acquiring that thing bring you greater happiness? Can you find happiness in being pleased for that person?

LOVE OR LOVING?

"Love is not only something you feel, it is something you do."—David Wilkerson

"It matters not who you love, where you love, why you love, when you love or how you love, it matters only that you love."—John Lennon

When can we say that we have achieved love? Often people proclaim "I found love" or "He is the love of my life." We set love goals for ourselves: "I want to be in love by the time I'm twenty." Or we become sad—"I lost my love," "I squandered my love on her"—as if there's a finite quantity of one's love. It's no surprise that contemporary Western culture diagrams this basic emotion as a noun—a "thing" that is exchangeable, acquirable, material, and thus assessable as desirable and valuable. We merchandize love with all its accoutrements. We

121

catalog the number of our "love" relationships and compare the number with that of our friends. Everybody wants love and goes to great lengths to "find" it.

Such an attitude is in keeping with the lifestyle many of us pursue, of acquisition and entertainment, the consumer culture so hard to resist. What do you like to do? The answer is more often *not* "tend my garden," "refurbish shabby furniture," "study ornithology," or "improve my guitar method," but rather "Shop 'til I drop!" Instead of doing, we seek to get. Supposedly the luxe brand handbag, perfume, shoes, or t-top will put us closer to also acquiring social admiration and thus "getting" love.

When we plan vacations, it's a scenario of "must go" or "must do." We buy adventures like notches on our belts, our bucket lists. We must ride all the roller coasters in the nation. We must visit the most exciting and expensive theme parks. We must find zip line adventures or tree-house dwellings. We must fly to an arena to see a miniature team play a game on a field far below. We believe having done this makes us attractive, maybe loved. We brag about how we've checked off prestigious activities— not achievements, but simply external activities. We try to gain attractiveness by playing the six degrees of separation game, pulling out a pic on our phone that we took with Don Ho as he walked by our table on a cruise, or buying a shirt with sequins and fringe that was (allegedly) worn by Elvis. And once we've told someone we've done this or we have had this brush with fame, in a sentence that takes two minutes to utter, then what? Who are we to gather love?

We are acquirers and consumers of the transitory, focusing on everything exterior and peripheral to personal value, which we then hope to cash in for the noun "love." And then we gloat that we are loved for our acquisitions—"My new girlfriend adores my car!"—and so advise others, "Honey, you need to find love." Perhaps instead we should struggle to seek out, like the legendary student who longs for a master teacher, the models of those who find the spark of value within and invest it in the world by the verb "loving." They may seem quiet or humble. They may not flaunt wealth or a luxurious lifestyle. They may not make a clamor, like the clanging of a cymbal, about the aura of loving they convey. They exude love daily by the habit of loving.

By loving. Love may be an emotion or experience, a noun we try to capture, but LOVING is a practice, a verb, a way of being. Love takes, while loving gives. Loving finds love along the way. And loving keeps no tally of the beloved. It is like a smorgasbord of nourishment for everyone. A serene and accepting smile, the tender touch of a hand on the arm or shoulder, warmth and joy in a gaze or glance—these are the gifts of loving. And they far outlast the hazy memory of the last roller coaster ride or football game.

Our age's paradigm of one who lives the process, the verb, of loving, is the Dalai Lama, universally admired and extolled. Tenzin Gyatso is the thirteenth of this designation dating back five centuries, believed by Buddhists to be the incarnation of a "realized" spirit who desires to return to the world to help humanity—that is, to be loving. With humble beginnings as the child of a farming family in a small town in Tibet, Gyatso was recognized as the holy incarnation at age two, and his life as the Dalai Lama began when he was officially installed at age five.

The selection process is based on a series of dreams, divinations, and signs, resulting in a test of the child-candidate. (You might recall the film "Little Buddha," which dramatizes such a process.) Gyatso, at two, was able to identify artifacts of the prior Dalai Lama, and so he was verified and later installed as the new Dalai Lama. At age six he began a rigorous program of study and was tested at age twenty-three, when he passed the exams earning the highest doctoral degree in Buddhist studies.

Study has given him a quiet life of meditation and contemplation, to be sure. Yet he characterizes himself as a poor and plain Buddhist monk. And he carries a mission, an obligation, to teach and exhibit loving. Those who have been in his presence say his loving aura can permeate an entire arena with its intensity. Such is the power and force of loving, which grows in potency the more it is practiced. Habitual loving is the closest we come to mortal holiness, for God too is Love. Our being is a product of loving. Our very creation comes from loving.

At home, the daily life of the Dalai Lama is that of a monk, indeed. As you would expect, he rises before dawn and engages in morning ablutions (self-care) and spiritual exercises of meditation, followed by a meager breakfast (nourishment) and physical exercise and then more study. In the afternoon he regularly meets with audiences of all religions. His life consists of a habit of loving, of reaching out with the practice and good news of love, a natural portion of his daily life.

The public obligation of a Dalai Lama is grounded in humanity, that which links and unites all people around the globe. His own serenity radiates from a self-aware centering achieved through knowledge and meditation, a unification of the many aspects of being-in-the-world. With a great sense of empathy, he hopes to help alleviate people's suffering, sharing through loving his own ways to discover the paths to inner calmness and peace, a true happiness. Such loving overflows the boundaries of a single philosophy or religion as a "universal value."

With full awareness the Lama encourages "the cultivation of warm-heartedness" and "compassion, forgiveness, tolerance, contentment, and self-discipline." I can think of no richer and rewarding life philosophy. If we were to fashion a reminder-poster to contemplate each morning, striving each day to practice these qualities, we could indeed find the serenity and happiness that cannot help but to overflow our own spirit into loving.

-PRACTICE-

WARM-HEARTEDNESS

FORGIVENESS

TOLERANCE

CONTENTMENT

SELF-DISCIPLINE

COMPASSION

Such serenity is not a magical gift; it begins with self-mastery. The HABIT OF LOVING must be grounded in self-discipline and exhibits itself in empathy, generosity, kindness, and humility. Its single byword is COMPASSION, which alters the self and can change the world, one loving act at a time. We may have few acquisitions; we may live a simple life. But we no longer need to search for love; we become part of cosmic love itself in our everyday habit of loving action.

LOVING EXERCISES

1. Take note each day of people you encounter who emanate love. Try to describe how their love touched you.

2. Choose a day and emulate the Dalai Lama for that entire day. Prepare yourself physically, mentally, and emotionally. Then go someplace social and simply be warm-hearted to everyone you encounter. Be aware of how this action affects your own well-being. (When I was a finalist for an important executive position and was to meet probably a hundred people separately with whom I would be working, I decided to try to make everyone I met that day feel like the most important person in the world. I got the job!)

3. As a meditation exercise, place the "PRACTICE" poster before you and work through each concept, exploring internally how to generate it through considering your own past experiences. Whom might you forgive? Who could you tolerate better?

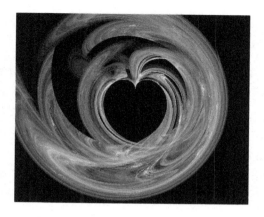

A PLAN OF ACTION FOR LOVING

"Love many things, for therein lies the true strength, and whosoever loves much performs much, and can accomplish much, and what is done in love is done well."—Vincent Van Gogh

Most of us are always making plans. I know people who by nature are speculative dreamers. Year after year they say "I wish I could . . ." or "I want to . . ." or "Wouldn't it be great if . . . ." At the other extreme are the pragmatists, who devise a simple plan, "Today I will accomplish this one thing," and they fret little about times beyond the job at hand. The rest of us might fall somewhere in the middle: we plan for the weekend or, months ahead, we schedule a yearly vacation and its itinerary. Some of us begin planning gardens in the midst of winter. We might set goals for ourselves, to lose weight or read a certain number of books or clean out all the closets.

On a larger scale, many of us consider having a grand plan for our lives. We joke with each other even into our golden years, asking "What do you want to be when you grow up?" Almost like a movie that flashes through our mind, a scenario of our future probably conforms to some kind of ideal fashioned through societal expectations and our personal histories and proclivities. Building on our upbringing, our location, our education and talents, we envision our life's path, the story of who we are to be. We create a narrative in which we can play the hero of our own lives.

As ethereal, nebulous, or even literary as this may sound, it is serious business. Without having to grapple with deeper philosophies and meanings of life, the nature of our creator, or why we are here, now, we all still live in a continuum of time that is marked by the passing of each day and limited in its span of years. On the one hand it serves us well to be fully in each moment, making time less pressing a concern by complete immersion in the experience of NOW. Yet this moment will pass and another will follow, and another and another. "Time creeps in this petty pace from day to day . . . ," notes Shakespeare's Macbeth.

Humans, as pattern-making animals, need to perceive a direction, even goals, destinations, the peaks and valleys of the full journey. We remember, and we plot out a future. If we fail to make these connections in time, we become like Macbeth with nothing ahead of us but a meaningless death, or Luigi Pirandello's "Six Characters in Search of an Author," or Jean-Paul Sartre's poor souls trapped in a purgatory with "No Exit." An existential crisis takes over our future, and, like Didi and Gogo in Samuel Beckett's "Waiting for Godot," we simply appear each day wondering what might befall us next.

These are frightening dramatic visions of the perception of a godless universe, caused in part by our failure to participate. Our life requires us to step into the starring role and to act mindfully with gusto. This is not a recommendation for recklessness. On the contrary, living our narrative fully necessitates active awareness and concentration. Throughout my life I've met several students, young and old alike, with both talent and aspirations, who somehow have not succeeded in marshalling their energies toward their goals. First, attention must be paid, and then we must focus clearly. Otherwise we are simply adrift and rue our lost opportunities in tragic retrospect.

Like our ancestors who gazed up at a story sky and connected the dots to draw recognizable images, we want to make sense of our lifeline. The more mindful we are about daily living, the easier this becomes. We try to recognize causes, and we strive for good effects. In eastern philosophy, the Tao is simply imagined: *a person on a path.* We traverse our path with a sense of past, present, and future. It is up to each of us to determine the details of that journey.

This truth is the opposite of the trendy pop philosophy asserting that "everything happens for a reason." We might try in retrospect to include unforeseen events in our personal narrative as propitious: if I hadn't been turned down for the job I thought I wanted, I would not have found my perfect position. And this was meant to be. Perhaps. But in actuality each of us on our own, with the fullest use of our mindfulness, must choose our path and then make sense of the pattern and direction of those choices. The responsibility belongs to us, and we can *choose* to live each day guided by love.

The feeling of love must come from inside. We can discover it through empathetic projection in a meditative practice based on the Golden Rule. If we think of others we know and their situations, if we remember past interactions and events, if we speculate on how we might respond "if . . . ," our measure of action should be "Do unto others as you'd have them do unto you."

Scenario visualization is excellent practice for spontaneous loving action. We do not naturally seek harm for ourselves; therefore, we will not harm others. We want to be treated fairly and respectfully. We hope for kindness in word and deed. We are moved by compassion and generosity. Often we experience what seems like karmic justice. As the popular saying reminds us, what goes around comes around. These actions we hope for in return should be part of our own plan for loving. The more we imagine ourselves acting with love, the more we will develop that capacity within ourselves. And the more we will receive love in return. It becomes a self-fulfilling cycle, always twice-blessed.

Empathy means "feeling into" another's situation. It's a version of "walk a mile in my shoes," but as an invitation rather than a dare. Everyone has a back-story that contextualizes their present action and interaction. If we are truly interested in our fellow humans and if we can feel compassion for everyone, we've taken the first steps toward finding that love in ourselves.

Instead of judging or insisting others act according to our expectations, we need to feel into their words, their lives. We can listen with empathy, truly trying to hear to respond rather than waiting for an opening to talk only about ourselves. Even conversation must be mindful. To love is to connect. We can try to be patient when speaking with others. Often silence is the best reply, with a projection of loving chi. We need not supply quick answers and remedies. Simple, patient loving actions carry an enormous potential and nourish both lover and beloved. These actions are twice-blessed.

Daily acts of love can begin with simply being kind. If we face each day with a sense of spiritual generosity, we too will find ourselves changed. To live in a state of loving is, in a sense, to find our place in the scheme of things and nestle in. Eventually, through a willful change in outlook, kind and loving action will come naturally and effortlessly. It will become our default position. We can move through the world with little suspicion or fear, little sense of competition or ego, a largesse of generosity. This must begin on a small scale, a commitment to love within ourselves as we brighten the corner where we are. But loving action has the power also to affect the entire world, one loving action at a time.

We've all met individuals who exude a noticeable aura of serenity and acceptance. We instinctively know that we can trust them. They've tapped into the grand creative force of love. As I admire these saints-on-earth, I use them for inspiration and try to work by their model. These saintly people seem refreshingly innocent and uncynical. Their serenity enfolds all whom they encounter in a comforting embrace of *caritas*.

When my husband was on his deathbed, my elderly neighbor wondered if she might visit him. Because he was a shut-in, she had not come to know him. At best they had exchanged waves of the hand in passing. I showed her into his bedroom and left to take a call. When I returned and entered the room, I felt the entire space filled with compassion. She was sitting on the bed next to him holding his hand, casting a profound look of love with her gaze. It was as if the Dalai Lama or the holiest of earthly persons had passed through. The room seemed illuminated by the light of her love, and it made a difference, then and there, and in the cosmic scheme of things, for all of us. Love can be palpable; it unifies us as members of the human family; it validates our time on earth. Loving kindness and compassion can also be contagious. My neighbor's display of loving has inspired me to be more compassionate.

I aspire to be like my neighbor. As we plan our life story, let it be benevolent, an adventure replete with propitious deeds. To plan a life—a future for us— that sees a path toward fulfilled living is always a way mindful of loving. Each step can be guided by love: awareness of the spark of creation within us, attention to self-love through self-care, and the focus of our intention to manifest love through our daily actions. Loving action brings together spirit, mind, and body.

After only a short time of practice, you will feel the results in your body and in your heart. Loving will change the nature of your being. Those who live each day guided by loving action are less prone to illness and to the vicissitudes, the ups and downs, of disappointments and mood changes. Look within yourself for that love. Feel it, tap into it, and know its power. As you traverse each day, others will notice and remark favorably. Your aura will glow strong and simply show. Throughout these chapters I've purposely used the words "we" and "our," including you, gentle reader, as a fellow traveler on a life journey replete with love. While each of us must find the path and follow it individually, we need not and must not see it as entirely a solitary journey. Frankly, love is what brings us together as walking partners and makes the travel worthwhile.

Through empathy with others, we live our life fully and also many lives in our one as we "feel into" their journeys. What a rare gift! This is another true irony of life, that to best fulfill our individual purpose, we must experience love together and follow its light. A cloistered love is always incomplete.

Think on these things, and be assured that I am walking my path alongside yours. I'm on the journey too.

LOVING EXERCISES

1. Locate in your mind someone whom you have dismissed because of a snap judgment: they're annoyingly talkative, they're smug and egocentric, they seem mean or rude, for example. We don't always instantly love everyone we meet. Now use your sense of empathy to "feel into" a day in their life. Do your feelings about them change?

2. Think of someone from your past who influenced you with loving attention. Describe your perception of this person's character. How might you emulate them?

3. Keeping in mind insights you've gained from this series of loving exercises, what exact steps can you take toward living a loving life? Precisely what measures will you take to tap into the power of love—and change your life for the better, forever? Write a motto based on your resolve and hang it in a prominent place. Sigmund Freud's was "Love, and work." And remember, my love walks with you on your journey.

"Love is, in fact, an intensification of life, a completeness, a fullness, a wholeness of life."
—Thomas Merton

"Love in its essence is spiritual fire." —Seneca

Books by Alexandra Mason

alexandramasonbooks.com:

"Lost and Found"

"Poems Along the Way"

"The Lighthouse Ghost of Yaquina Bay"

"Shakespeare's Money Talks"

"Shakespeare's Pipe"

"J. Carl Ellston of Exeter, Missouri"

"'A Handbook for Love' shares many glimpses of wisdom into the transformative power of love. It softly and thoughtfully invites us to love, simply love. May we all gain such wonderful insights into the joy of living and creating a life filled with hope, kindness, and serenity."—Dean Shrock, Ph.D., author of "Why Love Heals"

"What does it mean to love and feel loved? How can we break through a belief that we are not loved or are unlovable? In this wonderful little guide Dr. Mason has done what few of us are able to do: take a complex subject and present it in a way that we can feel as well as understand what she means. Through story, quotes, and a simple, straightforward style, we learn the answers to these questions and more - and through doing the practices she offers we get the deeper meaning. A blessing indeed! —Ruth L Miller, Ph.D., author of "The Science of Mental Healing" and "One Law: Henry Drummond on Nature, Spirit, and Love"

"Love is a word that gets used with different meanings which are often ambiguous. Here Dr. Mason explores the many facets of love, and with an emphasis on the practical application, she ends each chapter with loving exercises. A deep, thoughtful, and delightful book."—Brent Burford, J.D., facilitator of adult religious education

Made in the USA
Columbia, SC
06 December 2022

72421752R00085